STRENGTH in DIVERSITY

A Positive Approach to Teaching
DUAL-LANGUAGE LEARNERS
in Early Childhood

Lea Ann Christenson, PhD

Gryphon House

Bulk Purchase

Gryphon House books are available for special premiums and sales promotions as well as for fund-raising use. Special editions or book excerpts also can be created to specifications. For details, call 800.638.0928.

Disclaimer

Gryphon House, Inc., cannot be held responsible for damage, mishap, or injury incurred during the use of or because of activities in this book. Appropriate and reasonable caution and adult supervision of children involved in activities and corresponding to the age and capability of each child involved are recommended at all times. Do not leave children unattended at any time. Observe safety and caution at all times.

Table of Contents

Introduction

The weather is crisp outside and cozy inside on this late October day in Ms. Lara's kindergarten class. Ms. Lara has twenty-one children in her class, nine of them English language learners (ELLs) from El Salvador, Mexico, China, Ethiopia, and India. Cutouts of autumn leaves and pumpkins adorn the room. A few key common classroom items, such as scissors, desk, a whiteboard, window, door, sink, soap, and so on, have labels that include a picture, the word in English, and the name of the item in the languages of the ELL students. Near the carpet area where the children gather as a whole class is a display of books, both informational and fictional, on the topic of fall celebrations. Ms. Lara has been reading them to the children over the past two weeks. A careful inspection reveals that the books reflect the countries and cultures of all the children in her class, including a child who speaks only English and who just moved from the state of Hawaii. Included in the book selections are the cultural celebrations of Sukkot (Jewish), Nuakhai (Indian), Oktoberfest (Germany), Día de Los Muertos (Mexico), the Dragon Boat Festival (China), as well as a few books on the American version of Halloween. Ms. Lara focuses on the common themes of family and community across the celebrations.

While reading the books, the children notice that many of the celebrations include food. Following the children's interests, Ms. Lara focuses the science unit she is required to teach—the five senses—on the investigation of various types of fruit, both those traditionally available in the local area (three types of apples and pumpkins) and those she was able to obtain from the places the children's families are from: pineapples, guavas, lychees, and plantains. Under the supervision and direction of Ms. Lara, the children investigate the fruit by cutting them open and describing the sound of them being cut open and the colors, smell, texture, and taste of each. The children then record, analyze, and display their data on charts and graphs created as part of a shared writing lesson directed by Ms. Lara.

She used this lesson as an authentic opportunity to teach and reinforce writing the numbers 1–10 and recognizing words with short and long vowel sounds (part of her required math and language arts curriculum). All the children, including the new arrivals who do not yet speak or understand English and two children who have individualized education programs (IEPs), are able to fully participate because Ms. Lara models what to do every step of the way.

During center time Ms. Lara has the students apply and extend their knowledge of the five senses and fruits. She leaves the opened fruits in the science center for the children to continue investigating with magnifying glasses. Ms. Lara has created and provided copies of graphs with the pictures and the words for the colors and textures, and the children record their own data to indicate the color and texture of each fruit. In the writing center the new vocabulary words for the week—*pineapple, guava, pumpkin, lychee, apple,* and *plantain*—are posted on cards along with photographs of the fruit. The children refer to these word cards as they work on their daily independent journal entries. Next week, the focus will be textures and color words.

The block center has been converted into an agricultural warehouse where the children are learning how to move large pumpkins from one area to another using cooperation and an inclined plane. To aid understanding, Ms. Lara had interactively shown the children a video the week before and then modeled how to move large items with the help of an inclined plane. Photographs showing the process, along with simple text in English, Spanish, Chinese, and Hindi, are displayed in the block area. Greg, an English-only student who sometimes struggles to focus during circle time, is patiently explaining to Juan, an ELL student in the preproduction stage of English, how to best move the pumpkins from one area to another using an inclined plane. Juan listens intently to Greg, and they cooperate to move a large pumpkin. In the art center, the children are painting with red, yellow, orange, brown, and black, traditional autumn colors in North America. Photographs of landscapes painted by the artist of the week, Georgia O'Keefe, and works by last week's featured artist, José María Velasco, hang in the center to provide inspiration. Ms. Lara reads a short biography and describes the style and techniques of each artist during circle time each week.

The teacher of English speakers of other languages (ESOL) pulls a group of three students at the speech-emergence stage of English acquisition to reteach them the concepts they were learning (the five senses) and to reinforce their learning of English words and meanings of school routines. The Mandarin translator provided by the school system arrives to confer with Ms. Lara as they prepare for the conference with Biyu's mother later in the day. Ms. Lara and the ESOL teacher have noticed that Biyu is still very nervous at school, and they want to discuss this situation with her mother to better understand how to meet Biyu's needs.

A paper copy of the weekly class newsletter, distributed each Monday in print and electronic formats, hangs on the parent resource bulletin board near the door. Ms. Lara is able to use the district's resources to have the letter translated into Spanish and Chinese. For the other languages, she uses Google Translate (with a disclaimer apologizing for any errors Google may have made). The newsletter includes the curriculum to be covered for the week, class events such as birthdays and the birth of siblings, upcoming school-wide events with descriptions of each, as well as tips for how families can assist their children at home.

If you are picking up this book, chances are you did so because you are a teacher or administrator who has at least one young English language learner (ELL) (also referred to as a dual-language learner (DLL)) in your classroom or program. You may think the scenario on the previous pages is a work of fiction and not a description of a real classroom and that you have no idea how to achieve the same results Ms. Lara did. This book is designed to provide you with the tools you need to enhance, not reinvent, your classroom to support ALL the children, including ELLs.

The term *ELL* is gradually being replaced by *DLL*. In this book, we will use the terms interchangeably.

Working with Dual-Language Learners: A Welcome Opportunity

For many early childhood professionals, the prospect of having an ELL/DLL in their classroom may seem overwhelming because their university coursework did not include how to serve these children. You may have taken one or two classes on how to serve ELLs, or the most likely case, none! Even if you have taken coursework on this topic, you might still feel uneasy when you teach DLLs in practice. It is natural to wonder how, with all the demands you have on you as an early childhood educator, you can meet the needs of young DLLs while also meeting the needs of the rest of your students. You cannot rely on the fact that your prekindergarten through third-grade classes will have ESOL teachers to help you serve your DLL students; these teachers usually work with DLLs no more than thirty to sixty minutes per day. If you are teaching in a setting that serves children from birth to four years old or in a private preschool setting, it is very likely that your school does not have an ESOL specialist.

In that case, you are likely responsible for the DLLs for the majority of the instructional day, and it is your primary responsibility that all your students' needs—both those of DLLs and those of English-only students—are met in your classroom.

Having a DLL in your class is actually an asset. No matter your prior training or experience with young DLLs, this book will help you meet the needs of all your students and discover why having DLLs/ELLs in your class is constructive. In reading this book, you will understand the theories and strategies necessary to meet the needs of young ELLs are, for the most part, the skills you need to optimize instruction for all children. To serve ELLs, you do not have to create a new curriculum or implement different strategies; you simply need to shift what you are doing to maximize the effectiveness of your lesson plans for benefit for your ELLs. This book will provide you with a conceptual understanding of how to support ELLs in your classroom by building off what you already know about teaching. Then, you will be able to integrate this foundational knowledge into your current practice and make it your own, just as Ms. Lara did. For early childhood administrators, this book provides you the background in early childhood and second-language acquisition that you need to best support your staff and the children and families they serve.

So then, this book is for you, whoever you are and whatever role in early childhood education you play and wherever you live in the United States. No new or expensive materials are needed. You just need to know how to leverage what you probably are already doing so you can meet the unique needs of DLLs and maximize instruction for all the children you teach.

Overview of This Book

This book is designed to be an easy-to-use guide to help those in early childhood settings (pre-K through third grade) plan and deliver inclusive and effective lessons for all their students. The following is an overview of the rest of this book. In many cases, you will find that effective strategies for ELLs are equally powerful strategies for all the children in your class.

In chapter 1, we will take a look at current statistics of ELLs. We will investigate some of the backgrounds of young ELL students and dispel certain myths and misunderstandings about ELLs. In particular, we will investigate learning theory and how both English-only and ELL students acquire language.

Chapter 2 identifies research-based strategies across all disciplines and analyzes how these strategies are specifically beneficial for children who are English-only speakers as well as for children who speak a language other than English. In chapter 3, we will see those strategies in action as we read about a sample unit that illuminates the previous chapters. Chapter 4 explores ways to work with all families in general, with specific tips on how to support families of our ELLs. In chapter 5, we will see these strategies and approaches in action in a kindergarten classroom.

Terms Used in This Book

Before we delve into this book, let's take a look at the different terms used to describe children (and adults) who are learning a second language. The alphabet soup of second- (and first-) language learning can be confusing. Become familiar with these terms and refer to this list as you move through the rest of the book to reinforce your growing knowledge.

- **BICS:** Basic Interpersonal Communication Skills; the level of language for basic communication, such as that used for simple greetings, purchasing items at a store, and for occupations, such as gardener, construction worker, and so on

- **Bilingual:** the ability to communicate (understand, speak, read, and write) at a CALP level in two or more languages

- **CALP:** Cognitive Academic Language Proficiency; the level of language (understand, speak, read, and write) it takes to communicate and engage successfully in academic settings and for occupations, such as accountants, teachers, scientists, and business

- **Code switch:** the ability to switch seamlessly from one language or dialect to another, depending on the contexts (and sometimes within a single sentence or conversation)

- **DLL:** Dual-language learner, a person who is learning two languages (L1 and L2) at once. This is the case for many ELLs; they learn English at school and continue to learn their L1 at home. This term gaining in popularity and is used interchangeably with ELL.

- **ELL:** English language learner (see DLL above)

- **Emergent bilingual:** another term for DLL/ELL; a person in the process of learning a second language with the potential of becoming bilingual

- **EO:** English only; a person who knows how to use only English to speak, read, and/or write

- **L1:** language one; the language a person learns to speak from birth, also known as native language, mother tongue, or home language

- **L2:** language two; the second language a person learns to understand, speak, read, and write (Some people are very lucky and learn an L3, L4, and more!)

- **Monolingual:** the ability to speak, read, and write in only one language

- **Translingual:** the ability to use L1 and L2 as an integrated communication system to switch between an L1 and L2 and leverage commonalities in order to learn L2

CHAPTER 1

The Demographics and Culture of Dual-Language Learners in the United States

Who Are the DLLs in Your Classroom?

English language learners account for 9.5 percent (five million) of US public-school students (US Department of Education, 2019). Do you know the number-one country of birth for ELLs in the United States? Did you guess Mexico? China? If so, guess again—it is the United States. Most ELLs in public schools were born in the United States and are US citizens. In fact, among the children who are ELLs in pre-K through fifth grade, 85 percent were born in the United States, as were 62 percent of ELLs in grades 6–12 were (US Department of Education, 2019). They are the children of first-generation immigrants and have been taught a language other than English by their families.

Another misconception is that ELLs are only in border states, such as California, Arizona, and Texas. Of the student population of California, ELLs make up 20.2 percent; however, the largest growth in the ELL population in recent years has been in the Southeast. For example, in the Fairfax County, Virginia, public school system, more than half the total student population speaks a language other than English at home, including more than 180 different languages and dialects (Fairfaxcounty.gov, n.d.). Other states that account for the majority

A Word about Generalizations

Even though the majority of ELLs in the United States speak Spanish, a teacher cannot label a student as *Hispanic* and leave it at that. Spanish speakers come from more than thirty countries around the world, and the United States is actually in the top five countries that are home to Spanish speakers. Argentina, Chile, Cuba, the Dominican Republic, El Salvador, Mexico, the Philippines, and Spain all have majority populations that speak Spanish as their L1 (Simons and Fennig, 2017). The Spanish speakers from these countries are culturally very different from each other and should not be labeled together as *Hispanic*. This thinking also applies to children who come from countries in Asia, such as China, Vietnam, Thailand, or Japan. They should not be lumped together as *Asian*. In this case, in addition to very different customs, traditions, and geography, they also have different L1s.

Each child is unique, bringing individual experiences, preferences, talents, abilities, and interests. Students can learn English even if they do not completely acculturate into North American culture (Litwin and Smith, 2019). Celebrate each child's cultural and ethnic background, and look for ways to integrate it into the classroom. This not only complements their education in the classroom, but also gives all students the opportunity to learn more about a wide range of diverse backgrounds.

As educators, it our responsibility get to know the children we work with and to promote an inclusive space for all students. We will look at generalizations in more depth in chapter 4.

of ELL students in public schools are Illinois (9.8 percent), Florida (9.2 percent), New York (7.9 percent), and New Jersey (5.2 percent) (Blizzard and Batalova, 2019). In addition, some midwestern states, such as North Dakota at 115 percent, have experienced the largest percentage of growth over the last ten years. Chances are you will have the opportunity to teach ELLs no matter where you live!

The majority of ELLs in America speak Spanish, followed by speakers of Arabic or Chinese. In fact, ELLs in US classrooms speak more than 160 different languages (Bialik, Scheller, and Walker, 2018). Other common languages include Vietnamese, Somali, Russian, and Hmong (US Department of Education, 2019). Although the majority of ELLs speak Spanish, of those that come from countries other than the United States, not all of them come from Mexico. They come from a wide variety of Central American and Caribbean countries. Thus, the cultural context in which they speak Spanish is very different. This is similar to how people who speak English in the United States differ from those speaking it in the United Kingdom or New Zealand. All these speakers can understand each other; however, there is a layer of culture, vocabulary, and idioms that is not readily comprehensible.

Who Is Immigrating to the United States?

In 2017, only 13.6 percent of the US population was made up of immigrants. Of this number, 77 percent of them immigrated to the United States legally (Radford and Noe-Bustamante, 2019). Additionally, researchers project that by 2055, the number of Asian immigrants will surpass Hispanic immigrants (Pew Research Center, 2015).

In 2018, 27 percent of the people who immigrated to America were from South and East Asia (Pew Research Center, 2015). This is a slightly higher percentage than those from Mexico (25 percent). Table 1.1 will better illustrate the countries of origin of immigrants currently living in the United States as of 2017, which is the most current data available at this time.

Languages Spoken by ELLs in the United States

US Department of Education, 2016.

Understanding Linguistic Enclaves

Many newly arrived immigrants live in linguistic enclaves. A *linguistic enclave* is an area where there is a concentration of people who speak the same L1 and have either just arrived in the United States or were born to first-generation immigrants and who are learning English and American culture. My parents were from an area of Nebraska where most of the people were descendants of immigrants from Sweden and Denmark. My great-grandmother emigrated at age thirteen in the late 1800s from Denmark and lived in this enclave. She attended a church that worshiped in Danish, and most of the people living around her also spoke Danish. She learned English BICS and became a janitor at the post office. She remained at a BICS level of English until my grandmother started school. She then studied along with my grandmother from elementary school to college and obtained a CALP level of English.

Linguistic enclaves exist in almost every city in North America. For example, there are large Ethiopian populations in Los Angeles, California (Banach, 2005) and Seattle, Washington (Hinchliff, 2010). Many people of Somali descent live in Minneapolis, Minnesota. People from El Salvador have settled in Raleigh, Charlotte, and Greensboro, North Carolina in addition to the large metropolitan areas of Los Angeles and Washington, DC. In a large city near me, several generations ago, most of the residents of one section of the city were recent immigrants from Italy and spoke only Italian. Remnants of this linguistic enclave still exist in the form of well-established Italian restaurants, an Italian festival every spring, and a bocce court open to the community. You probably have a linguistic enclave near you, too. As you'll learn in the next few chapters, living in a linguistic enclave will strengthen a child's first language, thus strengthening their future level and competence in English.

It's Not Just about Language, It's about Culture, Too

Along with a language other than English, young ELLs come to school with rich and diverse cultural backgrounds. Keep in mind that children who speak the same language may not have the same cultural experiences. In fact, children speaking the same L1 can have very different cultures, just as a child from Alaska has a different culture and experience of America than a child from Florida. Although both children may speak English and be familiar with SpongeBob or Elmo or all the lyrics to the *Frozen* soundtrack, they likely have different cultures and experiences around traditions, climate, idiomatic language, clothing, and some food choices. Similarly, a child from Mexico and a child from El Salvador have had different experiences with traditions, foods, clothing, and idiomatic language.

In addition, children who come to America may have had experience with school but may not understand the nuances of American schools. Or a child may never have attended a formal early childhood school setting, or her native classroom setting may be very different from her new school. The food she encounters in her new school may be strange and unfamiliar. That being said, the child knows many things about where she is from that her

Cultural Disconnect: An Example

At an American elementary school serving a large population of ELLs from a country in Central America, the custodians complained that the children were leaving used toilet paper in piles on the floor beside the toilets. Luckily, one of the pre-K teachers at this school had traveled to this particular country on a short-term study-abroad experience and had worked with children in a small rural village. Upon her arrival to the village, she was told that the village did not have running water or plumbing. They showed her the latrine and told her not to put toilet paper down the hole under any circumstance, as it would disrupt the chemical breakdown of the waste. A trash can, emptied daily, was placed next to the seat for that purpose. If you were a child in the village who put toilet paper in the latrine, you would get in big trouble from your family because you risked ruining the ecosystem of the latrine. The teacher respected this custom and never threw toilet paper in the latrine during her visit.

She explained this fact to the other teachers and custodians at her American school. The next day the teachers went to the restrooms and demonstrated (with the help of a translator) to all the children—not just the ones who had come from Central America—the proper disposal of toilet paper. After this respectful instruction, there was no more toilet paper on the floor.

new teacher and peers do not. A child does not come to school as an empty bucket to be filled but as person full of knowledge and language. The teacher needs to connect to what the child knows and help her to grow and understand the new customs and culture of her American school.

Making Connections

As noted above, we now know that most young ELLs are born in the United States. Although the most prevalent native language of ELLs is Spanish, we know that Spanish speakers come from many richly diverse countries and cannot be generalized as one group. As we continue to learn about the ELLs in our classrooms, we need to be empathetic in our investigation to understand the unique differences in their cultures. Investing in DLLs' education will benefit the United States economy overall (Ross, 2015). Not only does education create better job opportunities for DLLs, but DLLs who are proficient in English are more likely to earn higher-paying jobs as well (Ross, 2015). English-only students benefit by working in class alongside children different from themselves, thus helping all students to think more critically; a skill sought after by employers in this global economy. As early childhood educators, we are gifted the opportunity of providing ELL students with an educational foundation that will open up academic and economic opportunities. Now that we know a bit about the characteristics of ELLs, we will review learning and language acquisition theories to understand how to best serve all the children we work with, both DLLs and English-only speakers.

Reflection: Who Are You?

Where are you from? When did your family come to the United States, or are you 100 percent Native American? Why did your family come to the United States? Was this voluntary or involuntary? What is your family's home language? What is your first language? What are your culture and traditions? What are, or have been, your family's challenges? What are, or have been, your family's successes and strengths?

CHAPTER 2

An Overview of Theories and the Stages of Second-Language Acquisition

At the foundation of high-quality and effective instruction for all children is a working understanding of child development and second-language acquisition theories. This chapter provides you with an overview of theories of learning that support all children. We'll explore conceptual understandings of the theories related to instruction and second-language acquisition for young children, as well as the research that supports multilingualism. Then, we'll conclude with a description of the different stages of second-language acquisition.

Benefits of Learning More Than One Language

To start, speaking two or more languages is a benefit, not a deficit. People who speak, read, and write in more than one language have a higher level of *neural plasticity*, which means their brains are better equipped to adapt to the environment and new experiences (Ramirez, 2016). People who speak, read, and write more than one language have better communication, memory, decision-making, and analytic skills, Ramirez notes. Did you know that people who speak more than one language are less likely to suffer from Alzheimer's when they are older (Ramirez, 2016)? This is due to the fact that learning multiple languages keeps more neurons fired up in the brain. At birth, we are capable of learning any language. As we get older, Ramirez asserts, the neurons used for other languages weaken (atrophy) and it becomes more difficult to learn.

Ramirez adds that this neural plasticity also increases the ability of being fluent in multiple languages later on. Children who learn two languages from an early age are more likely to have native-like fluency in each language, as opposed to adults who try to learn a language later on when their brains are not as elastic. Additionally, babies' brains "mold" to the language their caregiver speaks. A baby who hears only one language will become used to one language and parts of their brains will atrophy; whereas, a baby who hears two (or more) languages will retain the ability to learn two (or more) languages more easily due to their more elastic brains (Ramirez, 2016). Furthermore, learning another language alongside English does not make it more difficult for the child to learn English overall. Ramirez says that children who are bilingual can learn English just as quickly as children who are English-only learners. This is because having a complex vocabulary and content knowledge in L1 this will easily transfer to English. Babies and children who are exposed to more than one language can focus better than babies and children who are exposed to only one language (Bialystok, 2001). This is an important life skill because the ability to focus is the basis for all cognition.

Contrary to popular myth, babies and children do not get confused when they are learning two languages at once. Children learn how to easily code-switch and use the appropriate language with the corresponding person or context. For example, recently I was sitting at a meeting next to a woman who was talking about her grandchildren. Her daughter was teaching her children English, the paternal grandmother was teaching them Spanish, and this woman was teaching her grandchildren her native language, Korean. She said that her grandchildren, ages three, six, and eight, seamlessly flowed from one language to the other depending on whom they were talking to. She said the younger grandchildren sometimes used different languages in the same sentence; however, the eight-year-old had all the languages sorted out. These children were experts at code switching, as they knew which language to speak to which person.

The Foundation: Seminal Child-Development Theories

Here is a quick review of foundational learning theory, which should be the conceptual framework for all lessons for both English-only speakers and ELLs. Use these theories as a lens for your lesson planning, which will help you make sure that your lessons are developmentally appropriate for all your learners.

Piaget and the Four Stages of Cognitive Development

Jean Piaget, a Swiss psychologist, suggested that cognitive development occurs at four main stages of a child's life (Huitt and Hummel, 2003). His stages have stood up against repeated research across many cultural contexts. The stages are outlined here, followed by ways they can be applied to your teaching.

- **Sensorimotor Stage: Birth to Two Years Old:** During this stage, infants use their senses to touch, watch, and listen to the world around them to form an understanding of it. They do not understand symbolic representation, such as drawings or letters. Around seven months of age, they start to develop *object permanence*, the ability to understand that an object still exists even when they cannot see it. Babies enjoy peekaboo at this age for this reason. At the end of this period, children have some language skills; however, their main means of understanding the world is through physical connections (Huitt and Hummel, 2003).

- **Preoperational Stage: Two to Seven Years Old:** At this stage, language skills grow and develop at a rapid rate, and children start to understand the world at a symbolic level by playing pretend, drawing pictures, and talking about things that happened in the past. They cannot yet understand logic. Children are egocentric at this stage and can see the world only from their own perspectives. As early childhood educators, this is the stage the children we work with occupy. This stage is what makes our instructional strategies different from those of our peers who work with older children. Often, in an effort to prepare our children to be college and career ready, we are given the same content and strategies to use with our two- to seven-year-olds that teachers of older children are given. This is problematic because the strategies designed for older children will not work for our younger children, who are not at the stage of development to understand. Younger children will grow frustrated because they are not capable of learning in ways that older children can (Huitt and Hummel, 2003). They need hands-on, active learning through exploration. Thus, as early childhood educators it is often our job to take the content we are required to teach and deliver it with strategies which are appropriate to the preoperational stage of development. However, some content (long division, for example) is not developmentally appropriate to the preoperational stage and changing learning strategies will do little to assist children in learning the concept.

- **Concrete Operational Stage: Seven to Eleven Years Old:** At this stage, children are able to learn logical and concrete rules about objects, such as their weight, height, and volume. They master the concept of *conservation*, the idea that an object such as clay or water remains the same even if its shape changes (Huitt and Hummel, 2003).

- **Formal Operational Stage: Eleven Years through Adult:** At this stage, children and adolescents are able to demonstrate logical and systematic thinking to understand abstract concepts and solve problems. In addition, concepts learned in one area can be generalized and applied to another area. (Huitt and Hummel, 2003).

Piaget's Stages Applied to Your Classroom

If you are teaching pre-K through first grades, you are planning for children in the preoperational stage. If you are teaching first, second, or third grades, you are planning for the concrete operational stage. (There is some overlap, depending on each child's development.) If you are being pushed to do more "academic" content with your students, use the goals and objectives of the curriculum to design related lessons for children in the preoperational stage. By doing this, you can teach more sophisticated concepts at an appropriate developmental level. You are the early childhood expert and know how the children in your classroom learn. Lessons taught at a higher operational stage will not be understood and will be a waste of instructional time.

For example, let's say that you are expected to teach measurement as a part of the math curriculum. For pre-K and kindergarten students, this unit of study needs to start with nonstandard measurement to teach the concept of how to measure. Children can measure how long a desk is using their hands, the length of the room using their feet, how tall their friend is by using blocks from the block area, and the height of a shelf by using string. With physical interaction, children in the preoperational stage can understand the concept of measurement as it relates to their own world. When they move to the concrete operational stage, they will be able to comprehend numerical values and use standard tools for measurement, such as measuring tapes and units of inches and feet or centimeters and meters. Your students will have a better chance of passing the benchmark assessments, which usually follow this type of curriculum, if you, the early childhood expert, stay true to the objectives and modify your instruction to the developmental level of your students. This developmentally appropriate approach will benefit both ELLs and English-only students.

Vygotsky and the Sociocultural Theory of Cognitive Development

Born the same year as Piaget (1896), psychologist Lev Vygotsky believed social interaction influences a child's learning. So, he proposed a theory of cognitive development in which children learn through social interactions with more skilled individuals (McLeod, 2019). McLeod notes that the most popular part of this theory is the idea of the Zone of Proximal Development (ZPD). A child's ZPD is the point at which a child needs a little help to meet with success with a lesson or task. The help that a more skilled peer or adult (the "knowledgeable other") gives is called *scaffolding*. Learning should be planned for a child's ZPD. If a lesson is too easy and the child does not need any help, then the lesson is a waste of time because nothing new is learned. If a lesson is much too difficult and a child cannot meet with success even with scaffolding, once again the child learns nothing, so this lesson, too, is a waste of time. Lessons need to be planned in the sweet spot of the ZPD: not too easy and not too difficult, and achievable with scaffolding from the knowledgeable other.

Overall, Vygotsky believed humans learn through social interaction and through this interaction will become socially competent. This social competence is the foundation of linguistic, cognitive, and emotional development, because interaction with others is necessary to learning from a teacher and other skilled peers or adults. Vygotsky believed that children learn best in social interactions with the knowledgeable other who scaffolds them to the next level of learning.

Vygotsky's Theory Applied to Your Classroom

The idea of a knowledgeable other is where your grouping strategies come in to play. For first-, second-, and third-graders, after you teach a lesson and model how to apply what was learned, you can have them engage in independent practice in small groups. Be strategic in creating these groups. You can group native English speakers with your DLLs; the native English speakers will be the knowledgeable others for English language learning. For example, let's say you just taught a hands-on science lesson using real rocks, showed videos on different types of rocks, taught vocabulary related to rocks, and modeled how to group rocks by characteristic so the children could practice sorting them by attributes and types. The native English speakers will reinforce the English vocabulary and scaffold the DLLs in understanding by working together on the task at hand. In addition, because you made the content comprehensible with videos and real rocks, the DLLs will most likely be able to understand the concept of sorting objects by attributes and be able to group the rocks. Their content knowledge as well as their English is scaffolded as they move forward.

This is why lessons should be designed around two-way communication. Some forms of technology may be able to do this to some degree; however, the most effective knowledgeable other is the skilled human teacher who knows his students' abilities and interests and uses this information to create interactive lessons to move his students forward. Lessons in which young children can communicate with one another are beneficial as well, as they can scaffold peers' learning. This is effective instruction for all children, including English-only students and ELLs.

Gardner's Theory of Multiple Intelligences

Howard Gardner, a psychologist from Harvard University, created an inclusive theory that highlights a wide range of learning styles. Called the Theory of Multiple Intelligences,

Gardner initially defined seven ways in which he believes people can understand their world. (Note, this is not an exhaustive list as his theory is still evolving.) Incorporating these learning styles is beneficial for all learners, both English only and ELLs.

Table 2.1: Gardner's Multiple Intelligences

TYPE OF LEARNER	STRENGTHS
Visual-Spatial	Visual and spatial judgment
Linguistic-Verbal	Words, language, and writing
Interpersonal	Understanding and relating to other people
Intrapersonal	Introspection and self-reflection
Logical-Mathematical	Analyzing problems and mathematical operations
Musical	Rhythm and music
Bodily-Kinesthetic	Physical movement and motor control
Naturalistic	Finding patterns and relationships to nature

Gardner's Theory Applied to Your Classroom

Reflect on these learning styles as you plan your lessons, and make sure you plan activities across the day and week that embrace all of these learning styles. The following chart offers some ideas to get you started. Remember that humans seldom fit into such neat categories. Your students may exhibit characteristics of multiple categories to greater or lesser degrees. Also remember that students have a strength in one of more of these learning styles, even if they do not speak English.

Table 2.2: Gardner's Multiple Intelligences in the Classroom

TYPE OF LEARNER	IDEAS FOR INCORPORATING LEARNERS' STRENGTHS IN YOUR CLASSROOM	SAMPLE WHOLE-CLASS UNIT: POETRY
Visual-Spatial	Enjoy completing puzzles alone or in groups, building with various building materials, and working with maps	Poems are word puzzles. The act of constructing a poem is rearranging words in space and time. Encourage visual-spatial learners to create poetry (written or dictated) or read (or listen to) poems and look for the structures.
Linguistic-Verbal	Have superior memory skills and the ability to comprehend and compose written or spoken information	Post a poem of the week in your class that reflects the theme you are working on. Use the poem as a shared reading for the week. Send the poem home (in English and translated into home languages), and students can practice it for homework. Students can perform this poem for the class at the end of the study.
Interpersonal	Enjoy group work, often take leadership roles	Have your students write (or dictate) their own and group poems. For older students, explicitly teach different poetry forms, and then have them create poems reflecting these forms as a group.

TYPE OF LEARNER	IDEAS FOR INCORPORATING LEARNERS' STRENGTHS IN YOUR CLASSROOM	SAMPLE WHOLE-CLASS UNIT: POETRY
Intrapersonal	Are self-aware and enjoy time to create alone	Create a safe space for students to create alone and then share their work, and model for the students how to give meaningful feedback. For very young children, this can be as simple as using pictures of emotions faces to show the poem made them feel.
Logical-Mathematical	Have strong logic and reasoning skills	Ask the children to look for patterns of poetic language in the world around us. Children can write (or dictate) poetry about math and science. Encourage older students to find the poetic language of technology and the scientific process.
Musical	Perceive and analyze the world through sound. Incorporate songs or rhythms into lessons so students can retain content better	Have children put their poems to music, either familiar tunes or tunes they create.
Bodily-Kinesthetic	Are aware of and learn about the world through touch and movement. Incorporate movement activities in learning	• Have the children create dance moves to poems you provide or poems they create. • Perform the poems for others.

TYPE OF LEARNER	IDEAS FOR INCORPORATING LEARNERS' STRENGTHS IN YOUR CLASSROOM	SAMPLE WHOLE-CLASS UNIT: POETRY
Naturalistic	Love spending time examining and learning from the natural world around them. Outside play is especially important for these children.	Go outside and use the natural world for inspiration. Write and perform group poems. Write with sticks in the dirt, in the snow, or with mud.

Bloom's Taxonomy and Critical Thinking

Bloom's taxonomy was developed by a team of researchers headed by Benjamin Bloom, a psychologist at the University of Chicago, in an effort to help educators promote higher-level thinking in their students. The team defined three broad categories that they considered the goals of the learning process: cognitive, affective, and psychomotor (Bloom et al., 1956).

- Cognitive: remembering facts and information

- Affective: organizing and categorizing facts and information in different ways

- Psychomotor: analysis, synthesis, and evaluation

Bloom's taxonomy is often depicted as a pyramid. A foundation skill, such as remembering or recognizing, is at the bottom of the pyramid, and skills such as understanding, applying, analyzing, evaluating, and creating are on top (Learning Theories, 2014). The content we teach mirrors this taxonomy. Remembering the names of the letters of the alphabet is at the bottom and is generally easy, and evaluating which materials in the block area are best for building an arch bridge is at the top—and is more difficult.

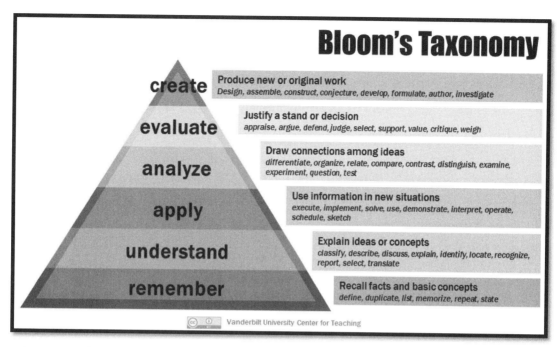

Source: Vanderbilt University Center for Teaching. https://cft.vanderbilt.edu/guides-sub-pages/blooms-taxonomy/

Bloom's Taxonomy Applied to Your Classroom

When planning lessons, start with the basics of remembering and scaffold to where students are answering questions and doing tasks that require analyzing. Then, give them opportunities to create from what they have learned. For example, when reading a book, children need to comprehend what the book is about, who the characters are, and the setting where the events take place. Next, they can begin to discuss what they've learned by reading (or hearing) the book and use the information in a novel situation. In the case of *The Three Little Pigs,* children can start by remembering who the main characters are, what the pigs do, what they built, and what the wolf does. Next, they can move to analysis—Why does the wolf want to blow the houses down?—followed by questions that evaluate: Which house stands up the best and why? At the highest level, the children would create their own houses and test to see if they could withstand the wolf's lethal blasts.

This was a quick overview of the basic learning theory that supports instruction for all the children you work with, English-only speakers as well as ELLs. Now we turn to theory that is specific to the needs of a child learning a second language.

Second-Language Acquisition Theories

Jim Cummins conducted the seminal research in the area of second-language learning. What follows is a summary of his theories. With a working knowledge of Cummins's theories, you will be able to modify instruction for all your students, especially ELLs.

Basic Interpersonal Communication Skills and Cognitive Academic Language Proficiency

If you have learned a second language yourself, or if you have worked with DLLs, you may have a hunch that there are different levels of language. Cummins developed the theory that there are two levels of language learning: basic interpersonal communication skills and cognitive academic language proficiency.

- **Basic Interpersonal Communication Skills (BICS):** This is the level of language used in simple social situations: for example, "How are you? Nice weather we are having!" or "What is your name?" and "May I go to the bathroom?" in a classroom setting. This level is used to complete simple tasks, such as buying groceries: "Do you have any bananas? How much does this cost?" For adults and older children, it can take up to two years to reach this level of language proficiency. Younger children, however, can reach this level more quickly. People with a BICS level of language can function in daily routines and social situations. Adults can engage in occupations, such as house cleaning, assembly-line work, or construction. Children can engage in simple conversations with peers, such as, "Let's play," or "May I use the red crayon?"

- **Cognitive Academic Language Proficiency (CALP):** This is the level of language it takes to be successful in school. It can take three to five additional years after BICS mastery to reach this level of academic language. In school, students at this level can learn any complex academic content, such as reading, writing, and math. Adults can engage in occupations that require an academic level of language, such as teaching, law, or science (Frankfurt International School, n.d.).

The time it takes to acquire an L2 depends on many variables: the circumstances of arrival, the education level of the parents, the parents' income level, and what resources a family has access to. Note that all of these variables equally apply to English-only students, too (The Bell Foundation, 2017). For students with at least two to three years of L1 schooling in their home country, the stages generally last five to seven years. If the student has received no schooling, it could take as long as seven to ten years (The Bell Foundation).

Cummins's Iceberg Analogy

Cummins (1994) used an iceberg analogy to explain how a person's L1 supports the acquisition of L2. More than 87 percent of the volume of an iceberg is underwater (Zoeller, 2015). What is visible is only part of the totality. This analogy works well for language learning. On the surface, it looks as though the two languages are completely dissimilar. However, if we look deeper, we see that there are similarities.

First, when a concept is learned in one language, the person does not have to relearn the concept. He just needs to learn the L2 vocabulary for the concept. For example, once you have learned the life cycle of a butterfly in L1, you do not need to relearn that concept in another language; you just need to learn the L2 vocabulary.

Come with Me to Codepres!

Guess what! It is the year 2060, and we have been invited by the government of Codepres to set up an early childhood center. If you forgot, Codepres is a planet similar to Earth in a galaxy discovered a few years back. The only problem is that we speak only English, and the people in Codepres speak Codepreslian! When we first arrive, we will live in our English-speaking enclave. Every day we go out and start to learn Codepreslian by taking classes and interacting with Codepreslians. After a while, we master our BICS and can conduct simple business, such as buying groceries and having basic conversations with Codepreslians about the weather. We enjoy Codepres; however, every evening we relax in our linguistic enclave speaking English with one another and sharing our daily experience and reminiscing about our time on Earth. Some of us have children; because we speak Codepreslian only at a BICS level, we speak our L1 (English) to our children. They learn a rich L1 of English at both BICS and CALP levels.

The children know all about the world where they are living now and about the world we left at a CALP level of English. We read to our children often. Once they go to formal schooling, they speak only a bit of Codepreslian but have very rich (CALP) English. The Codepreslian teachers have a solid L1 foundation to build on, and after five to seven years our children have BICS and CALP in both English and Codepreslian. They have excellent critical-thinking skills, and when they are ready to enter the workforce, they are top candidates because they are bilingual and bicultural. As for us, we still are most at home in our L1 of English and may always be, but after five to seven years we have CALP in Codepreslian. Some of us feel comfortable enough to move out of our linguistic enclave. Others have finished the project we were hired for and return home to Earth.

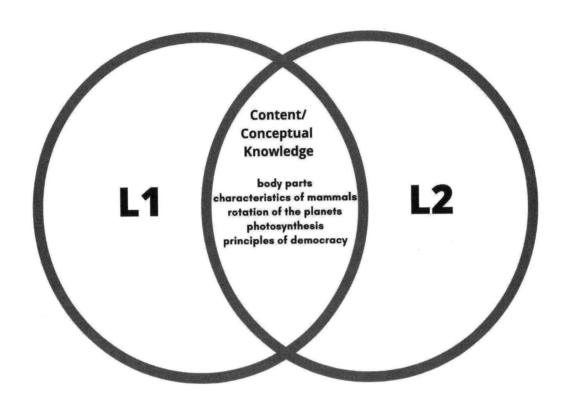

Second, many languages have strong similarities. Some languages are closely related, and as such, a person can rely on his knowledge of L1 to deconstruct his understanding of L2. For example, Spanish and Italian are very similar. If a person is fluent in Spanish and knows the Spanish words for fish (*pescado*) and cat (*gato*), then it will be easy for him to learn the words in Italian: *pesce* and *gatto*. Languages that are farther apart linguistically and or graphically, such as English and Mandarin or English and Hebrew, would have less in common "under the water."

Another way to explain this concept is the *common underlying proficiency* (CUP). Prior to Cummins, the other theory was that we have separate "balloons" in our brains for each language and they do not intersect. Cummins explained that we actually have one balloon in our brain that holds all our knowledge and then multiple channels (languages) to access that knowledge. CUP explains that you do not need to reteach a child a concept he already understands in his L1. Instead, you simply need to provide the L2 vocabulary. This is because many words or concepts are translingual and exist or have the same meaning in many languages (Turnbull, 2018). *Translingual* is a relatively new term used to describe bilingual individuals' ability to understand concepts across languages and switch between languages in their minds (Nagy, 2018).

Many teachers wrongly assume that if students speak their L1 in the classroom, they will not be able to learn English. On the contrary, if you are teaching a lesson about community helpers and you allow the children to use their L1 to discuss what they have learned, and you send information in your students' L1 to their homes so their families can support what you are teaching, your DLLs will have a much richer understanding of what community helpers do, and they will bring these concepts with them as they learn English. Using their L1 helps them learn English faster because it allows them to clarify anything they might not understand and leads to a more complex understanding.

Many teachers wrongly assume that if students speak their L1 in the classroom, they will not be able to learn English. In reality, using their L1 helps them learn English faster because it allows them to clarify anything they might not understand and leads to a more complex understanding.

This fact also explains something very important. If at all possible, children need to continue learning in their L1 while acquiring CALP in L2. If they do not, then they are at risk for falling behind grade level in content knowledge (The Bell Foundation, 2017). Since teachers usually do not have CALP in the L1 of their students, it is up to the family to continue developing the child's L1 while the child develops CALP in L2. As we have learned, it can take five to seven years for a child to develop CALP in L2. Therefore, families should be encouraged to teach their children in L1.

Cummins's Quadrants

Cummins has one more bit of theory that will help us plan effective lessons for all young children. It has to do with learning language with "context-reduced" or "context-embedded" activities.

Overall, *context-reduced activities* rely on the learners' knowing the language without the use of anything in their environment, such as visuals. These activities can be either cognitively demanding or undemanding. Cognitively undemanding, context-reduced activities require knowledge of a language, but overall the task is still fairly easy to complete. An example of this would be having a telephone conversation about simple concepts, such as, "How is the weather?" Conversely, cognitively demanding context-reduced activities are nearly impossible to complete without full comprehension of a language. These tasks are made even more difficult by the fact that there are no context clues to help language learners figure out what is being asked. Examples of these activities would include standardized tests and teaching CALP without the use of visuals, demonstrations, or hands-on learning. Whenever possible when teaching DLLs, we need to avoid context-reduced instruction.

Context-embedded activities are not exclusively dependent on knowing a language but are contextualized. Like context-reduced activities, these tasks can be either cognitively undemanding or cognitively demanding. For cognitively undemanding context-embedded tasks, not much is learned by completing the activity. An example of this would be coloring a page in a coloring book. The learner doesn't need to know a particular language to complete the task; however, not much new is learned by simply coloring. On the other hand, examples of cognitively demanding context-embedded activities would consist of science experiments or demonstrations. Often, the learning from these activities is complex (CALP); however, since these activities have many context clues in the form of lots of visuals and are hands-on, the content is learned and mastered at a CALP level in spite of the level of L2.

Table 2.3: Cummins's Quadrants

	CONTEXT EMBEDDED	**CONTEXT REDUCED**
COGNITIVELY UNDEMANDING	Easy with clues • Game of Duck, Duck, Goose • Coloring a coloring page • Cut-and-paste art project	Easy with no clues • Telephone conversations on simple topics, such as "How is the weather?"
COGNITIVELY DEMANDING	Tough with clues • Science experiments • Demonstrations	Tough with no clues • Standardized tests • Teaching CALP content with no visuals, demonstrations or hands-on learning

Optimally, all our instruction should be demanding and context embedded for our DLLs. This will help them learn grade-level content while acquiring English. Many English-only students benefit from this approach as well. Our goal, then, as teachers is to teach cognitively demanding lessons in a context-embedded manner.

Stages of Second-Language Acquisition

Think about how babies learn language. As was discussed earlier, babies are in the stage Piaget defined as the sensorimotor stage, and they explore the world and learn language by using their senses to watch, listen, feel, and taste to understand. By being engaged with the world and the language around them, they start to make their own utterances. The people around them engage in interactive conversations with them and explain the world verbally and through hands-on interaction. When caregivers play and show babies the world, they are engaging them in real-life work activities. For example, a baby learns about water not just by seeing water and hearing the word *water*. He also learns about water by being immersed at bath time and engaging with a loving caregiver who helps him safely explore the water and gives him a vocabulary to explain what he experiences. Learning a second language should be no different.

People learn a second language just as a baby learns his first language, with the exception that they have prior knowledge from the first language and a foundation on which to build the second language. So, it is important to remember that the theory of language acquisition applies for anyone trying to learn a second language. Imagine if you were placed in a foreign country. You too would go through each of the following stages until you reached advanced fluency.

Second-language acquisition looks the same in everyone, regardless of age. As an early childhood educator, it is helpful when lesson planning to reflect on these stages to know what to expect from your young students and how to help scaffold them to the next level. Young children typically pass through these stages more quickly than older learners, mostly because their brains are more plastic. Remember, however, there are many other variables, such as poverty, level of L1, and family circumstances, that affect how long it takes to learn L2. English-only learners may experience these circumstances as well, and their learning can be affected.

Table 2.4: Stages of Second-Language Acquisition

STAGE	TYPICAL LENGTH	TYPICAL ABILITY
Preproduction	0–6 months	• Cannot verbalize in L2 • Is able to display slight comprehension through nodding "yes" and "no" • Is able to display slight comprehension through drawing and pointing
Early production	6 months–1 year	• Verbalizes one or two familiar phrases • Still has limited comprehension
Speech emergence	1–3 years	• Has fairly good comprehension • Can say basic sentences • Speech is filled with grammatical errors • Does not yet understand humor
Intermediate fluency	3–5 years	• Makes few pronunciation errors • Displays obvious comprehension of language
Advanced fluency	5–7 years	Comprehends, speaks, and writes on a level similar to a native speaker

(The Share Team, 2018)

Let's step into Ms. Kiara's second-grade class to put this information into action. Ms. Kiara's classroom is a hive of activity during her literacy-center time. Luz, who was born in the United States and is a native Spanish speaker, has acquired advanced fluency in English. Luz is in the literacy center seamlessly code-switching between Spanish and English as she works with Sara, a native English speaker, and Yamila, who is at the speech-emergence level of English. Yamila arrived from El Salvador in the middle of kindergarten. In her home country, she did not attend school regularly because school was a two-mile walk from her home. The assignment in the writing center is for the students to create a chart using the results from an experiment on flight conducted the day before. The students made and flew paper airplanes and measured how far they flew based on the elements of construction. Luz helps Yamila in Spanish and Sara in English when they do not understand what to do.

At the small-group literacy table, Ms. Kiara is working with five students who are recent arrivals to the United States: Bai and Chen were born in China, Dunia in Syria, Mateo in Colombia, and Dalaja in India. They are all at the preproduction stage of English. Ms. Kiara is reviewing a book on air travel that she had previously read to the whole class. She has two sets of word cards with targeted academic vocabulary, such as *jet, pilot,* and *helicopter,* including clear photographs for each word. The group is playing a matching game, and Ms. Kiara is encouraging the children to repeat the words after her when they make a match.

Types of Programs

Now that we have reviewed learning theory and have learned about second-language acquisition theory, we'll turn our attention to some supports for DLLs in schools settings.

- **Bilingual support:** instruction of academic content takes place in children's L1 until they acquire CALP in L2. The teacher in a program of this kind is required to have native fluency in both the L1 of the children and English.

- **English speakers of other languages (ESOL) support:** assists children whose L1 is not English and who are not fluent in L2 (in this case, English); usually supports children until they develop BICS in L2

- **Push-in support:** English as a second-language (ESL) specialist goes into the class to assist the general education teacher for short periods each day

- **Pull-out support:** ESOL teacher pulls DLLs out of the general-education class

- **Newcomer program:** usually for middle- and high-school students, to assist with BICS and assimilation to US school and culture

- **Translators:** people who have native fluency in English and the L1 of the children and families who can provide written and oral translation

Programs vary from state to state and between public and private settings, so not all of these supports may be available in your area or school. Keep in mind, although your DLL students may receive extra support, you still are the number-one person in their school life and their biggest source of help in the classroom.

Lau v. Nichols

Non-English-speaking students in San Francisco, California, sued the San Francisco Unified School District (SFUSD) for the lack of supplemental language instruction. Instead of being taught English, some of these students had been placed in special education classes, and others had been forced to stay in the same grade for years. The students alleged that the lack of supplemental language instruction amounted to a violation of the Civil Rights Act of 1964, which bans educational discrimination, and the Fourteenth Amendment, which requires the states to provide equal protection under the law to all people, including all noncitizens, within their jurisdictions. In 1974, The US Supreme Court ruled that, because the SFUSD received federal funding, it had violated the Civil Rights Act and was required to provide "meaningful education" to all students in the district. This meant that the district had to provide supports to bring the students' English language ability up to the level that they could participate meaningfully in the education offered by the district.

Bilingual Support

In a perfect world, all children (English-only and DLL) would be in bilingual programs. Their instruction in academic content would take place in their L1 until they acquired CALP-level proficiency in L2. At the end of five to seven years of support, all children in the program would be completely bilingual. These types of programs take place in a few states and most commonly teach English and Spanish or English and Mandarin. The problem, of course, is that children come to US schools speaking more than one hundred languages, so schools would need materials in each language. Teachers would need CALP-level fluency in both English and one of those one hundred languages, because a child needs to be taught at a CALP level, not just a BICS level.

Since the ruling in *Lau v. Nichols*, English learners are guaranteed a meaningful education (US Department of Education, 2020). The majority of funding for ELL programs comes from state and local sources (Sanchez, 2017); federal funding accounts for only about 11 percent of school districts' spending. However, the US Department of Education estimates that as many as half a million students do not get any services at all (Sanchez). Because of this, the types of resources available may differ greatly from one district to another and one state to another. Bottom line: You, the general educator, are the "teacher of record" and ultimately responsible for the success of all your students, both dual-language and English-only learners.

ESOL Support

ESOL programs assist children whose L1 is not English and who are not fluent in their L2 (in this case, English). ESOL programs usually support children until they develop BICS in their L2, not until they develop CALP in L2. The ESOL teacher should work with the general-education teacher to find out what is being taught in the regular-education classroom and then preteach or reteach the grade-level content to the DLLs. This approach supports DLLs in learning English and keeping up with grade-level content. The ESOL teacher also may work on curriculum specially designed for DLLs, to help them become familiar with US culture and routines in school.

Push-In and Pull-Out Supports

With push-in support, as in ESOL, an ESL specialist goes into the class to assist the general-education teacher. Typically, this is just a short period of time every day.

In pull-out support, just as it sounds, an ESOL teacher pulls DLLs out of the general-education class to work with them.

Making Connections

The content we've covered in this chapter is usually covered in several university-level courses, so we have covered it widely but not in depth. Hopefully, this chapter will spark your interest to learn more. Keep these theories in mind as we move forward. They will act as a framework as we discuss the effective principles of instruction for DLL and English-only students. These theories will really come to life in chapter 5 through the lens of a sample unit. Overall, remember that when these theories are employed, instruction will be maximized for *all* students, no matter what their L1 may be!

CHAPTER 3

Putting Theories
into Action

Now that you have an overview of the theories relevant to meeting the needs of DLLs (and English-only learners too), this chapter will provide you with some general examples of how you can put these theories into action in your classroom. You may already be implementing some of these strategies. If so, that's wonderful because you do not need to start over when serving DLLs. Sometimes all that is needed is a slight shift in practice, which will enhance learning for your English-only students as well.

Create a Welcoming Environment for All Children

The first step is ensuring that your classroom is a place where all children feel safe, loved, and accepted. Without this important step, none of the others principles and strategies will be effective. The most important thing you can do is build a unique relationship with each and every child. Outwardly demonstrate respect and acceptance for all children, and be authentically warm and welcoming. A child can feel it if she is not wanted or accepted by her teacher. When you have a caring tone and an authentic smile on your face, the children will feel secure and ready to learn.

Ms. Jen is a teacher in a private half-day preschool program. About half her class is comprised of DLLs, mostly from southern India and Ethiopia. At the beginning of the school year, several students struggled to transition to their new school environment. The preschool director was aware of this situation and made sure to start her day in the class as an extra pair of hands to reassure and give extra guidance to the students and parents. Every day, Ms. Jen stands at the door and personally greets each child by name. She waves to the parents and smiles and has a quick conversation about simple concepts, such as the weather. After several days the parents feel secure knowing their children are well taken care of and no longer linger at the door. Inside the room, Ms. Jen's assistant, Ms. Marie, helps usher the children to their cubbies, smiles, and helps them put away their backpacks and coats. The cubbies are labeled with the children's names and photos. Ms. Jen, her assistant, and the director are tuned in to the emotions of their students and take extra time to connect with any children who seem upset. Once they have taken the time to make sure all the children (and their parents) feel secure, they start the activities for the day.

It is well researched that "classrooms characterized by warm and engaging teacher-student relationships promote deeper learning among students" (Jones and Bouffard, 2012). Make sure you show through gestures that you care. You will be modeling for all your students how to care for others.

Ms. Aimee teaches kindergarten in a Title I* school. She noticed that her DLLs often did not eat the free meals offered by the school. When she asked a few students who spoke the native language of the DLLs why this was happening, she found out that the children were not familiar with the food. Ms. Aimee made a point of purchasing breakfast and lunch at her school and then sitting down with the children to eat. She brought in pictures of how the food was grown and made, and she warmly encouraged the children to try the food. It did not take long for the children to begin enjoying their school meals.

Know the Children in Your Classroom

Make time to get to know the children as individuals. The more you know about your students, the more empathetic you will be, and in turn, you will be able to build authentic relationships. Make sure you connect with each child every day. This connection, in addition to actively doing a little research about your students, will help you build unique relationships with the children in your care. Strong relationships will help you avoid misunderstandings and support children to solve small problems before they turn into big ones. In chapter 4, we will explore specific strategies for learning about the backgrounds of all your students and their families.

If you're unfamiliar with Title I of the Elementary and Secondary Education Act, its purpose is to provide funding to assist schools that have high percentages of children from low-income families.

Mr. Tim, a preschool teacher in a Head Start program, recently welcomed a new student named Binsa, who arrived from Nepal. He noticed that Binsa always takes her shoes off at the door, which is a problem because school policy states that children are to wear shoes at all times. With the help of an interpreter, in this case a fifth-grade student, Mr. Tim found out from Binsa's aunt that it is customary in Nepal to remove one's outdoor shoes before entering a home or a classroom. With the permission of Binsa's guardian, Mr. Tim provided Binsa with a pair of shoes from the school clothing exchange that she could wear while in class. This little extra proactive effort on his part helped Binsa to feel welcome and part of the class instead of feeling like an outsider and helped her comply with school policy.

Learn a Few Common Words in Each Child's First Language

Another welcoming tip is to learn a few common words in each child's L1. Fluency does not matter: your attempts will show the children that their first language is of value and something to be proud of. This is easy to do in the age of technology. Online tools such as Google Translate include an auditory feature so you can hear how words are pronounced. Other online resources such as Learn Spanish Today offer a list of common words, including greetings, along with pronunciation guides. Learn some basic words, such as *mommy, daddy, bathroom, hungry, thirsty, water, hurt, happy, sad, sick, scared,* and *play*. Write each word in the child's native language and in English on a card, and include a picture (a realistic photograph, if possible) to illustrate the word. This card collection will help you remember the words, and the child can use it as a tool to communicate with you by pointing to the pictures on the cards. Consider giving each child her own personalized set of cards as well.

Our names are the cornerstone of our identity as individuals. As you would for all children, learn your students' names and how to pronounce them. If possible, find a native speaker and ask for help with pronunciation. At the very least, use Google Translate. Continue to keep trying to pronounce names correctly, and verbalize that you are trying; do not just pass over the name and move on. Also, do not Americanize children's names, as was often done in the past. This practice is denigrating and does not value the child for the unique individual that she is. By learning children's names and words in their home languages, you will serve as an excellent role model. Learning a new language is not easy, and anyone who tries needs to be supported in the effort.

Expect Your DLLs to Participate

Expect all the children in your classroom, including the DLLs, to participate and engage in learning, and give them the tools to do so. Once, I worked next door to a second-grade teacher who was very empathetic and caring towards her dual-language students; however, her empathy led her to a place where she did not expect her DLLs to participate. She would often have the DLLs work on simple puzzles while the rest of the class was engaged in a lesson. She did not want the DLLs to "feel bad" about themselves because they could not understand the lesson. It is actually possible the DLLs felt bad about themselves because they were excluded.

All DLLs will be able to participate in your lessons if you give them the tools to be included. Modify your instruction with the strategies in this book and your DLLs will be able to fully participate and learn important grade-level content knowledge while acquiring English. Allow children to collaborate in their native language as they learn new concepts and skills. Remember, concepts do not have to be relearned in a second language, only the L2 vocabulary. Do not baby your DLLs because you feel sorry for them. Instead, empower them with tools for learning.

Teach DLLs about Your Classroom Norms

To help children feel comfortable, DLLs will need to learn about US school culture, practices, and customs. You will also need to explicitly teach them what school is like in your unique classroom. These practices may be so commonplace to you that you do not even realize they are not common practices everywhere. Often, we are so close to what we do, such as our routines for going to the bathroom, eating lunch, and communicating with families, that we forget that practices vary from teacher to teacher, classroom to classroom.

Invite a person you are very comfortable with to observe your classroom and find the "hidden curriculum" (Siraj-Blatchford and Wong, 2006). Preferably, this person would be someone who has spent time in a school in another state or country. This person could even be a noneducator who is not familiar with your school's practices. What is most important is that it be someone who can give you an objective snapshot of what she sees in the classroom.

Invite her to ask questions about your practice and routines. From this information and perspective, you will learn which practices you need to explicitly teach to DLLs and any students who are new to your classroom and school.

Explicitly teaching your classroom's routines and culture will help new students and parents feel welcome. These routines and information are called *cultural capital*: the knowledge of the norms and practices of a certain culture that can be leveraged to meet with success in that culture (Moore, 2004). If we are not aware of the cultural capital and do not teach it to students who are not familiar, we may be creating inequalities.

Discovering the Hidden Curriculum

Think about your routines, expectations, and practices from the perspective of someone who is new to your classroom. Consider things such as the following:

- Classroom expectations:

    » What are the expectations for lining up to either come into or leave the classroom?

    » How do you greet the children? How should they greet you?

    » How should the children behave upon entering the classroom? How do they know, for example, where they are to store their belongings and what they are to do first?

    » How do the children learn about the daily schedule?

    » What are the expectations for whole-group lessons? Do children raise their hands to be called on?

    » How do students obtain supplies, such as pencils, paper, and glue, to complete independent work?

    » What are the routines for small groups?

    » What is expected of the children working independently? Where do they hand in completed work?

    » How do they learn about playground expectations? learning-center expectations? mealtime expectations? bathroom expectations? What are the procedures for washing hands?

    » What are the routines for working in learning centers, such as art, blocks, and dramatic play?

    » What are the routines for cleaning up?

    » How do you expect the children to express their needs to you?

    » Do you help children, especially DLLs, engage in play with their peers?

    » What are the routines for leaving the classroom at the end of the day? For example, how do children get their coats and put them on, take home homework, stack chairs, and so on?

- Outside the classroom:

    » What are the routines on the playground?

    » How is lunch obtained in the lunchroom? How does the process work if a child brought her lunch from home?

continued on next page...

- » What are the expectations of students at assemblies?
- » What are the expectations for using or checking out materials from the media center?
- » What can you add? What is unique about your school?

- Communicating with families:

  - » How should families contact you when there is an issue with, or a question about, their children? Should they call? send you an email? text you?

  - » Do families need to come to the school to meet with you in person for conferences? If so, do you offer meeting times that are convenient for the families? Do you offer other ways of meeting, such as via Zoom, FaceTime, or another tool? How do you communicate these expectations to families?

  - » Are families expected to have access to the internet, perhaps to get and send emails, read online newsletters, or log in to a school portal? If so, do you offer support to families who either do not have access or are unfamiliar with your school's way of doing things?

  - » Are communications offered in the families' home languages? Is there someone on staff who can support families in communicating with the school?

- Understanding school policies:

  - » How are families informed of school rules and policies?

  - » Are they informed in their home languages? Are the signs posted in the school and classroom in the home languages of the families you serve?

  - » Do families have specific opportunities and encouragement to ask questions?

We cannot expect people who are new to our environment to ask questions in order to understand what is going on, as they may not feel comfortable enough to ask or even know what to ask. As the school year moves on, be prepared to learn from all of your students and their families as much as they learn from you. Add what you learn to what others have told you. Next year, perhaps you will be the one leading other teachers in their quest to understand all of their students.

Focus on Communication

Create a classroom community where all students learn by communicating (Rietveld, 2010). Think Vygotsky: Children have the ability to learn from one another, and they do this through social interactions. The more social interaction children have, the more socially competent they will become. English-only speakers can help DLLs with English, and DLLs can help all your students with conceptual knowledge via hands-on classroom learning activities. In this sense, having DLLs in the classroom is a gift because they offer a unique learning experience for all the students that would not be possible without them. Foster an environment rooted in peer support where the children can use each other as resources. In doing so, you are not only facilitating their learning but also building their career-readiness skills. Engraining respect for and appreciation of diversity, inclusion, and team-building values within your students from an early age will certainly help them succeed in the future.

In retrospect, first-grade teacher Ms. Jayla realizes how her teaching has evolved since she started teaching in a suburban area where a third of the population are DLLs. In this school, there are twenty-seven languages represented. She remembers that, in the beginning, the majority of her lessons were whole group, and she did all the talking. She used few visuals, and her lessons often lasted thirty minutes. More often than not, the children—both DLLs and English-only learners—began misbehaving and did not learn enough to apply her lessons to their independent work. Over time, through trial and error, reading professional resources, and daily reflection on her practice, her teaching evolved to become communication focused. Now, in addition to respecting her students' developmental levels, she does not ask her students to sit in one place for more than twenty minutes, and her lessons are interactive group conversations. She introduces concepts with the support of realia (real, authentic objects) and visuals and has the students engage with the lesson by giving physical responses, such as a thumbs-up when they hear the academic vocabulary of the week or holding up number cards to give the answer to math problems. She poses questions both easy and difficult (think back to Bloom's taxonomy), and she has the children turn and talk to one another before she calls on students to answer before the group. She makes sure she calls routinely on all students and uses equity sticks to keep track. By allowing students to do more of the talking, she has discovered that they often deconstruct concepts in ways that she would have not thought of and that are more comprehensible to the rest of the class. At times, the learning is facilitated by students in their L1. The result is engaged learners who take responsibility for their learning and are more able to transfer that learning to their independent work and lives. Another positive outcome, Ms. Jayla reports, is that she rarely has to redirect a child for misbehavior during these reconstructed lessons.

A number of techniques can help you facilitate communication with and among your students. Slow your pace down a bit when talking with your DLLs. Talk distinctly and enunciate clearly. However, do not slow down or enunciate so exaggeratedly that you distort what you are saying. Speak in a normal tone and volume; do not talk more loudly. Talking loudly will not make your students understand you better, and it might frighten them.

Wait time is your friend. When you ask a question of the class or an individual, pause for fifteen to twenty seconds. This wait time allows your students to process what you have asked. We as teachers are often uncomfortable with silence and fill it with our own utterances. By staying silent for several beats, you give your students time to process their thoughts and put together a response. This strategy is important for all students, but especially for DLLs. Not only do DLLs need time to consider what you've asked, but they also need time to think of their response and the words to say in English. If students are still not responsive or on the right track after you have given them some wait time, they may benefit from gentle scaffolding. Add a few extra questions that can help lead them to the answer.

Turn and Talk: a technique in which the teacher poses a question and then has the students turn and talk to the person next to them discuss the answer. The teacher explicitly models this process at first so the students know what to do. Each group shares an answer at the same time to keep them accountable, and then the teacher calls on four or five groups one at a time for answers that can be deconstructed as a group. This technique keeps the children engaged and allows all of them to participate with all of the questions, not just the one they are asked to share.

Equity Sticks: ice-pop sticks or craft sticks labeled with each student's name and kept in a container. The teacher pulls one out and calls on the student whose name is on the stick. Teachers can either put the used stick in another container, so she makes sure all students are called on before starting over, or she can put the stick back so all the children know they might be called on for every question. Regardless, the teacher needs to keep track mentally of whom she has and has not called on to make sure she calls on everyone routinely.

Ms. Maritza, a first-grade teacher, uses this strategy throughout the day. During math instruction she makes sure to pause for ten to fifteen seconds before calling on a student, even when there are many hands in the air. She knows that Omari knows the numbers in English but he needs a bit of time to process, so this extra time benefits him as well as others. Her students also know that she does not always call on the students with their hands up, so they need to be prepared. Ms. Maritza tailors her questions to each child to maximize her potential for success. For instance, she knows that Jahel, who arrived a short time ago from Iran, is very good at addition but is not yet confident in the English names of numbers. She invites Jahel come to the board to solve the problem and then asks another student to read the problem and answer in English.

Create Opportunities for Cooperative Learning

Assign each dual-language learner a buddy who speaks the same native language, if possible. They can rely on each other to translate as they acquire English. This way they can reinforce the content they are learning in their stronger academic-level native language while they build their abilities to understand and speak in English. Some people think allowing a child to speak their native language will take away from their ability to learn English. Remember Cummin's Iceberg: once a person learns a concept, he does not have to relearn it in another language; he just needs to learn the words for it in another language.

In addition, assign each DLL an English-only buddy to help show her the routines and procedures of the classroom. This will provide the DLL with an English-speaking role model and the English-only buddy with an opportunity to work with someone with a different perspective. This way, students at a more academic English level can solidify their skills by modeling their English to students who are learning the language. Cooperative learning experiences in which students are placed in small groups and each student is given a specific job foster these important skills through communication.

Ms. Jane, a pre-K teacher, taught a whole-group lesson on color names. She introduced the primary colors—red, blue, and yellow—and demonstrated how to mix the colors to create orange, green, and purple. She then showed the children how to match the color words with the colors. For a cooperative small-group activity, she strategically grouped the children. In this case, she made sure her DLLs were in groups with English-only learners. Each child was given a specific job that Ms. Jane had demonstrated within the group:

- **Supply person** to get the supplies

- **Color mixer** who would mix the colors

- **Label person** who would match the word cards to the colors

- **Reporter** who would report the results to the whole class

She gave the children time to cooperate and mix their own colors, first orange, purple, and green and then they could experiment to make any color they wanted. The children matched the color words to the colors and, with inventive spelling, wrote the words for the colors they created. All the children were successful in mixing and labeling the colors because they worked together cooperatively and followed Ms. Jane's explicit modeling. They all participated because each child had a specific job. Even children with very limited English could participate because the lesson was hands on and the other children in the group could provide support.

For each cooperative lesson, Ms. Jane makes sure to rotate the jobs so everyone gets a chance to get supplies, label, report the results, and so on. This way one child cannot do everything while the rest sit by and watch. Ms. Jane provides extra support for children who are shy or who have limited English so all children grow in confidence and meet with success.

Be Intentional about Your Small Groups

Think strategically about how you create your small groups across the instructional day.

Sometimes you will want all the DLLs together so you can preteach (sometimes called *priming*) and reteach content. DLLs who are grouped with others who speak their L1 can discuss the concepts in their L1 and translate for each other. This will help mitigate the possibility of their falling behind in their content knowledge. They are able to share knowledge about the content and engage in social interaction during whole-group instruction.

You can also sometimes include English-only learners who would benefit from preteaching and reteaching. Having DLLs in groups with English-only learners gives the DLLs role models of their own age. If you have assigned seating in your room, make sure to change it every month or two. This gives all children a chance to work with a wide variety of other students. We all have something to learn from others. As students work with a variety of peers, they will gain more perspectives from one another. This will help them become adaptable to many social environments and work with a wide variety of people.

All students, but especially DLLs, should be grouped by their level of English so they can receive precise and strategic instruction in English while learning the grade-level curriculum. At some times, you will teach to the needs of the entire group. At other times, you will teach to small groups and individuals to meet the specific needs of each student.

Respect Children's Language Acquisition

It is crucial that you respect a child's native language as an asset and not a deficit. Respect the process of acquiring an L2. Making mistakes when learning a language is how children learn. Just as you would do for a child learning her first language, gently correct errors that DLLs make. For example, if a child is learning the names of farm animals in English and calls a cow a *horse,* you would not say "No, that is a cow." Instead you would say, for example, "That does have four legs and lives on a farm, but that is a cow (point to picture of a cow) and this is a horse (point to horse). Remember the cow gives milk and the farmer rides the horse." Don't expect too little out of them, but do not expect too much either. Scaffold, scaffold, and scaffold them in their zone of proximal development. Take note of what children can do and have them model for the rest of the class, then lead them to the next step of the process. For example, when teaching procedures for routines, make sure to model and model again. Students can use their L1 to ask clarifying questions of a same-language peer. In this way, they will better understand what they are doing and whether they are doing it correctly.

At the beginning of the year, for example, explicitly teach routines such as how to get ready to go home for the day. Provide a chart of visual cues to help the children remember what to do. Think through each step of your expectations and exactly how you want the children to complete them. First, model the steps for them, and then have other children model. Finally, have a few practice runs before it is actually time to leave the classroom. Do not just say, "Put your chair on your table." Model the behavior as you say the instruction. Verbally deconstruct exactly what you expect, having a few children model one at a time how to put the chair up and correcting them if necessary. Then have the whole class practice while you watch and provide feedback. Be sure to give frequent, specific, positive feedback when the children execute the routine successfully: "Parveen, you did a great job putting your chair on the table. The legs are facing the ceiling, and I did not hear a sound." Parveen gets to feel proud for a specific accomplishment, and the other children are reminded in a positive way exactly how to execute a task. If a student has had difficulty remembering how to do a task, give specific praise as soon as she does it correctly. You may need to reteach routines after long breaks from school. The time put in to teaching routines is gained back by the time saved in an efficiently run classroom. This process works for teaching content as well as routines.

Model independent work and check for understanding before the students work independently. Spot-check to make sure they are on track; if not, stop and reteach what is expected of them until they can demonstrate it correctly. Use students who are on track as models. Often DLLs are doing the correct thing; be sure to use them as models as well.

For example, after you explicitly teach and model a lesson on one-to-one correspondence for your whole group of kindergartners, make sure to check for understanding once the children are back at their seats. Check to make sure your DLLs understand the concept even though they may not yet have the English vocabulary to express it. Then, even if a child is at the early stages of learning English, she could demonstrate her understanding for those who do not yet understand the concept. Not only will this empower the child who is learning English, it will also demonstrate a strength-based perspective to the rest of the class.

Just as you would not water down your curriculum for your English-speaking students, do not do so for DLLs. Recently, I learned that some educators believe that *developmentally appropriate practice* means a watered-down curriculum. This is far from the truth. Developmentally appropriate practice means employing teaching strategies at the appropriate grade or age level, including using academic language that meets the developmental level of the learner. This usually means hands-on learning in authentic contexts (remember Cummins's quadrants). English-only learners can benefit from the strategies used with DLLs, so they can stay on grade level as well.

Build Background Knowledge and Academic Vocabulary

It is impossible for a child to build CALP in an L2 without having strong background knowledge and academic vocabulary. Consider this: if a child moves from the city to the country, she may be wrongly labeled as *behind* because she has never seen or had experience with farm animals. She may not know anything about livestock but may know all about the public transportation system, how to read bus or metro maps, and how to purchase a ticket for a ride. On the other hand, a child moving from the country to the city may know all about farm animals, what they eat, how much they should weigh to go to market, and the going rate per pound, but may be "behind" in her knowledge of the city public transportation system. Sometimes our curriculum is dependent on a child's common knowledge of the world around her, when in fact, children can have very different experiences before they enter school. This disconnect in prior knowledge is exacerbated when a child is coming from another culture or country. To help build all your students' knowledge, it is important to investigate the backgrounds of all the children and then fill in their knowledge base where needed. Then, you can scaffold student learning and discuss what they have learned. Once you discover what a child knows, you can supplement this knowledge with the knowledge of your classroom, community, and required curriculum.

For instance, before a new unit of study, supply the needed background knowledge with realia, books, and videos. Often, teachers reserve a field trip as the culmination of a unit of study. Instead, consider using a field trip to provide hands-on background knowledge *before* the unit of study. It is easier to learn academic vocabulary with hands-on experience. Where do you typically go on field trips—the zoo, aquarium, museum, fire station, or park? How could an experience there provide background knowledge for your students before your unit of study? It is much easier to understand the different shelter and food requirements of mammals and reptiles if you have observed their habitats firsthand. Children will then have rich experiences on which to build concepts and academic vocabulary.

Support Children's Oral Language to Increase Their Vocabulary

Oral language is the foundation of written language and competent readers. Oral language is learned best in social contexts and is characterized by an extensive vocabulary that reflects rich, wide, and deep content knowledge. It is easier for all children to learn new vocabulary if it is taught in an authentic context. Choose books around themes, and strategically decide what academic vocabulary to focus on. By reading together with students, you foster communication and can scaffold their understanding of words they do not know. Students will start to develop their thematic vocabulary in an authentic way. Picture books can be helpful tools for older students as well as young or DLL students because the pictures can convey complex ideas and academic vocabulary. Remember: A rich oral language is the foundation of reading and writing.

Optimize Your Classroom Environment

Create a classroom that optimizes students' learning from the physical environment.

- Place posters filled with words and visuals, especially when teaching new vocabulary, to help students deepen their understanding of concepts.

- Post word banks of vocabulary related to the theme and content being taught. Do not overdo it: six to eight words per theme is more than enough for preschool or kindergarten children. Better to cover fewer words in depth so the children master them than to cover many words that the children do not master. Post the words along with corresponding pictures to support understanding, and change the words with each new unit. You can include "sight words" or frequently occurring words, but they, too, should be rotated rather than remain in a static display throughout the school year. Refer to the word wall frequently as you teach concepts.

- Make your own symbols to represent common words, such as *recess, bathroom, drink, lunch,* and so on. Anything to help students visualize and act out the concepts that you teach will be helpful.

- Consider labeling objects and spaces in the classroom in the L1s of the children. Include each word in English, along with a photograph. Remember that most young children do not yet know how to read; these labels can support emergent literacy lessons and show respect for languages other than English. But do not overdo it; be strategic and use the labels as teaching tools. If you do not refer to the labels and teach from them, then they are just visual noise.

- Use labels and pictures to assist children in navigating the room and knowing where things are kept. All the children in your classroom will be empowered by being more self-sufficient.

- Use picture cards at centers illustrating what the children are supposed to do. Remind them of the procedures and rules. When possible, consider using real photographs to avoid confusion.

- Change your signs as your themes change and when children do not need the labels to know where to put materials.

The strategic use of labels will give all children a respect for other languages and the value that each child brings to your class. Not only will this show respect to your DLLs and make them feel more included, but it will also help your English-only students' brain development. Overall, respecting the languages in your classroom will teach all students to respect language differences.

Read Aloud

Reading aloud is an essential element of a literacy program in an early childhood classroom. Here are a few tips to assist your DLLs and English-only learners who could use extra support.

- **Preview:** In a small group, preview the text to introduce new vocabulary and concepts. Provide extra visuals and realia to support understanding.

- **Read:** Before reading to the whole group, ask the children to watch out for a certain target word or concept. For example, you could ask them to look for the main character or words that express emotion. Tell them to make a certain gesture for the target concept or word, such as asking them to make horns on their heads with their hands when they see the moose, or to point to their mouths when they hear the word *delicious.* As you read, make sure the children discover the word and do the gesture. This will allow all the children to be active during the reading, and they will know exactly what you want them to learn from the reading.

- **Ask questions:** Ask questions while you read. Craft questions that your DLLs can answer. For instance, if you have a child in the preproduction stage of language learning, you can ask, "Who can point to the bear?" and have the child do that. The DLL will know what a bear is from the work you did in previewing the book. Children should be able to answer these questions quickly since they already have a strong understanding of what you are teaching them. As they advance in proficiency, you can increase the difficulty of the questions you ask.

- **Review and reinforce:** After reading the book with the entire class, reteach the concepts and vocabulary in your small groups. Make sure to go over pictures and focus on targeted vocabulary. Have children create their own picture books around the targeted academic vocabulary.

Idiomatic Language

We use idiomatic language all the time without realizing it: "It is raining cats and dogs." "Break a leg!" "Kill two birds with one stone." Idioms vary from region to region and country to country. Be aware of the idioms you use and explicitly teach them to the children. Even native speakers often don't understand idioms. For a fun exercise, try saying some idioms and asking the children what they think the idioms mean. You'll get some creative answers! When older children become more fluent in English, have them share idioms from their L1 with the class.

Contextualize Instruction

Have you ever encountered a word in isolation whose meaning you did not know? Have you seen a word that has multiple meanings and been confused about which one was intended? Once the word was used in context, however, it made sense. Take a look at this example: *wrest pin*. Do you know what that is? How about after you read this sentence: The piano tuner tightened the string around the wrest pin. Could you now make an educated guess? If you have some prior knowledge about stringed instruments, you might quickly surmise that the wires of the instrument are wrapped around the wrest pin to tune the piano.

Contextualization is important for all children, especially DLLs. Teach new vocabulary within the context of themes and the content of the curriculum. For example, when teaching words about animals, teach them in their specific context. To teach about farm animals, use photos and videos of animals commonly found on farms, along with images of a barn, a pasture, a pig sty, a horse stall, and other relevant images.

Young children, in particular, learn with their whole bodies. Act out words. For example, to teach directional words, show the children the words and have them act them out: *jump up, move down a step, lean to the right*, and so on. You could also use the vocabulary in songs that incorporate actions, or you might role play different classroom activities.

Allow plenty of time for learning thorough play. Engaging in play around themes is an effective way for ELLs to learn naturally and authentically as they play with their peers. (Remember what is and is not a theme; see page 77.) Hands-on games and activities outside, in the block area, in the dramatic play area, in the science center, in the art center, and elsewhere should support the theme and academic content and vocabulary. Add relevant realia to the centers for the children to play with. For example, if you are studying farm animals and farms, add toy farm animals and equipment to the block area (Christenson and James, 2015). If you are studying grocery stores, add toy foods, empty food packages, shopping carts, and cash registers to the dramatic play area. Label the items and use the words in context: "Brianna, I see that you and Marisol are shopping. You are using a shopping cart to gather apples and cereal."

Whenever possible, have the children do activities themselves. Give them hands-on opportunities to connect language with actions. It is the process and not the product that they learn from.

For example, after modeling a whole-group experiment on the properties of objects that float versus objects that sink, have the children replicate the experiment with new items in the science center. Be sure to model thinking aloud as you narrate what you are doing during the experiment and the thought processes you are using to determine whether the objects sink or float. For independent small-group or pair work, provide each group with a tub of water and novel objects (each labeled with its name) to investigate on their own. Provide the children with clipboards, pencils, and a data sheet with two columns—one labeled *float* and the other labeled *sink*. Encourage the children to write the name of each item on the data sheet and to check whether it sinks or floats. After they have finished, have them report their data to the whole group. Activities like this are concrete and foster communication skills between peers.

Use realia whenever possible to support children's learning and relate the concepts you are teaching to real items. If you cannot bring in the real item, use video (avoid cartoons) and photographs to support children's understanding. Use words to label and describe the objects.

- **Fruits and vegetables or other foods:** Be aware of fruits and vegetables the students have never seen. If possible, include ones from the children's cultures that native students may not have seen. Families can help you with suggestions of foods to include. Be aware of any food allergies your students may have.

- **Construction tools:** Include items, such as hammers and saws, if possible. Of course, enforce safety rules!

- **Lab equipment:** Provide beakers, scales, magnifying glasses, droppers (pipettes), and test tubes.

- **Community helper hats:** Bring in actual construction helmets, firefighter helmets, chef hats (toques), and so on. Avoid using knock-offs; try to get the real thing.

- **Kitchen equipment:** Provide real baking pans, cookie trays, pots, lids, measuring cups, sieves and colanders, mixing spoons, spatulas, whisks, and measuring spoons.

- **Plants:** Have nontoxic plants in the classroom, such as herbs, spider plants, succulents, jade plants, dracaena, Chinese evergreen, and bamboo.

Think Aloud and Model

Narrate what you are doing with the children. Say it out loud, explain step by step, and demonstrate what you are doing. Use the academic vocabulary you have selected for your theme. Take a look at this example of how a teacher thinks out loud when he is teaching.

TEACHER: Today, when we go to the science center, we are going to continue our *investigation*. Remember that word, *investigation*? Here is a photo of a *scientist investigating* the number of legs *insects* have (points to photos of scientist and insect). Look at the *scientist* (points to woman in a white coat looking through a *magnifying glass* at an *insect*).

Look at the *magnifying glass* (holds up word card with picture and word magnifying glass in addition to the actual magnifying glass). This is the *magnifying glass*. It is a tool scientists use to *investigate*. It allows them to see details they cannot see with just their eyes. Look what the *magnifying glass* does (holds magnifying glass above insect so that the children can see the legs better).

You are going to be *scientists* today (holds up word card with picture and word *scientist*) and use a *magnifying glass* (holds up the *magnifying glass* labeled with the words *magnifying glass*). You are going to look at the five *insects* under the magnifying glass and count the legs (holds up card with the word *insect* and picture of an insect).

Next, you are going to be a *scientist* and record your results as we did when we *investigated* pumpkin seeds. Watch what I do. I am looking at the *insect*. I am counting the legs: one, two, three, four, five, six (points to each leg as she counts). On my record sheet, I am going to write the number six next to the picture of the first insect (writes a number *6* on the record sheet). Remember how we write a six. Start at the top and swing around like this. Use your finger to write some sixes in the air with me.

Teach and model routines so that the ELLs can become self-sufficient even before they are fluent in English. Modeling once will not be enough. Model two or three times with a final model done by a student before allowing students to do it on their own.

Here are some more examples of times when you can model and think out loud:

- During procedures and routines, such as how and where to store supplies, how to line up for recess, and so on

- During shared writing, when reading and teaching with print large enough for the children to see and interact with

- When deconstructing comprehension in an interactive read aloud

- In the block center, after reading a book on bridge building, build a bridge model with the children and think aloud with them

- In all centers, such as dramatic play, art, math and manipulatives, writing, sand and water, science, and so on

- During self-help skills such as washing hands or tying shoes

- In helping your students enter into learning and play with others

Support Children's Choices

Foster children's motivation by offering choice, autonomy, and a voice in what they learn. Whenever possible, allow students to follow their interests and determine the direction of a unit of study. For example, let's say you want the children to master the ability to characterize objects based on their attributes. It does not matter if the students do that through a lens of a unit on insects or the solar system; they can learn this important science concept within any unit your students find interesting. Or let's say you read a book to your first-graders about elections, what they are, and what they're used for. You invite a local elected school-board member to meet with the class to discuss how people can work together to solve problems. The children then discuss the problems they see in their school and choose one to address. They decide to take on the problem of running in the hallways. They work together to think of some solutions. Then, they make posters explaining why running is a problem and what to do instead. They then march through the school hallways during lunch, carrying their signs. DLLs of all levels are involved in making signs and marching throughout the school to make the entire school community aware of the problem and the solution.

Caution: Do Not Make a Caricature of Culture

St. Patrick's Day is more than a day of leprechauns and wearing green. Cinco de Mayo is not even a major holiday in Mexico. Chinese New Year is more than firecrackers exploding and dragons marching in the street. Do some research. Talk to people from that culture or country (if possible) and learn what the major holidays are and authentic ways to celebrate. Also, do not limit the coverage of diverse cultures to certain days. Such limiting tends to minimize the importance of these celebrations and trivialize the cultures. The study of people from different backgrounds should be the backdrop to your entire year. Also remember that just because a child might be from a certain country or culture, it does not mean the child is the "poster child" for that region. Be sure not to overgeneralize. Gain a personal understanding of each of your students' unique cultures before incorporating their culture into the classroom.

Encourage Children to Share Their Cultures

Every child comes to your classroom with a unique family culture. As a teacher, allow students to share their cultures to facilitate learning. This is a great way to show respect and value across the classroom and will also help ELLs develop their language skills. Make sure to have pictures reflective of the cultures in your room and of others around the world. A librarian once told me that books should be mirrors to reflect who the children are. Children should be able to see people like themselves reflected back to them as role models. Books should also be windows, tools for children to learn about all the different cultures in their class and around the world. Share bilingual books, audio books, and videos with all the children in your class, both in the L1 of your ELL students and in other languages. This will validate the L1 of the children in your class and help all children understand that English is not the only language in the world.

Don't forget that English-only learners have individual cultures too! Sometimes we lump everyone together, but not every child in your class has the same cultural experiences as others who speak the same language. Students benefit from hearing about other languages and cultures to gain a wider perspective and help with their own brain development.

Encourage children to share their own unique stories in developmentally appropriate ways, such as orally, in drawings, and in writing. These are examples of social and emotional learning that will lead to stronger academic learning. Make sure to establish regular opportunities for students and families to share their cultures. You can have a special week for this but, once again, make sure it is a theme that runs through your entire year. This is time well spent that will pay off in the future and educate the whole child.

Focus on What Children Can Do

Always remember, the level of English a person knows is not a measure of her content knowledge or critical-thinking skills. We tend to focus on what children learning English cannot do; instead, we need to focus on their strengths. All children come to school with strengths. It is up to us to discover what they are and build on them. Take, for example, a child in a rural community in Nepal or El Salvador. Some of these students had to walk long distances and navigate difficult terrains to attend school, or perhaps they know how to act around an open fire in their kitchen, while some of the children in your class cannot put on a coat by themselves because their families have done everything for them.

Ms. Rachel, a first-grade teacher, discovered that Beatriz, her DLL from Ecuador, was the best student in the class on a unit on money. It turned out her family ran a small store in the town they were from, and Beatriz knew how to count out change in US currency. After a bit of online searching, Ms. Rachel discovered that the currency used in Ecuador is the US dollar (this is true of about a dozen countries around the world, including El Salvador and Zimbabwe). She also noticed that Carlos from Nicaragua was quick to understand the unit on money. His mother had sold produce at a roadside stand, and he had helped to collect money and make change. The conceptual knowledge Carlos had about money was easily transferred to US currency. Ms. Rachel noticed that her American-born first-graders were having a harder time with the concept of money, because their parents often used debit or credit cards and they had little experience with bills and coins. Thus, in spite of the fact they were not yet fluent in English, Beatriz and Carlos had more prior knowledge about money as well as the strongest conceptual knowledge, due to their firsthand experiences.

With each of these unique backgrounds come unique strengths that other students, or even you, may not have considered. DLL students are learning to speak multiple languages where most children and teachers in the classroom cannot say the same. DLL students bring so much to your classroom, and it is important that they are able to share that with you and their classmates. Find out what each child in your classroom can do and celebrate it. Speaking their L1 is an asset. Celebrate this and make sure to elevate their L1 to the same level of importance as English. By allowing children to elaborate on their unique skills and backgrounds, it opens up the door for better language acquisition with authentic diversity and learning for all students.

Leverage Technology

When used strategically, technology can be a useful tool with working with DLLs. To be strategic, technology should be used to solve a problem (Christenson and James, 2020). For example, if, during a unit to discover how plants grow, children are using a measuring tape to find how much their plants have grown and a pencil and paper to record their findings, then the measuring tape, paper, and pencil are considered technology. However, if children sit in front of a screen passively watching a video on how plants grow, the screen and computer are

Evaluating Online Sites for Teacher Resources

Websites for teacher resources, such as Pinterest and Teachers Pay Teachers, contain some wonderful ideas. However, you are the expert for your own students and are now armed with your renewed overview of theory. Make sure the ideas you gather from these websites embrace the concepts we explored in chapter 2 and are adapted for your unique students. An easy litmus test is to ask the following questions:

- Does this activity teach my students something new or reinforce knowledge just learned?

- Are the children solving a problem when engaged in this activity?

- Is this a meaningful hands-on activity?

- Are the children learning or reinforcing academic vocabulary when engaged in this activity?

- Are the children exploring higher-level questions, such as how and why, when they do this activity?

Some craft projects are very cute and clever; however, upon close examination, students do not learn anything new by completing them nor do they solve any problems or learn or reinforce academic vocabulary. When children glue precut ears on a precut polar bear face, they're not building or reinforcing their knowledge of polar bears. Skip that craft project and pick from the many interactive, hands-on learning activities that teach and reinforce knowledge.

not technology. It is not about how sophisticated and expensive the technology is; it is about how it is used.

Think about how tablets can be a tool. They can be used to collect data by taking pictures. You and the children can utilize online sites for translation. You and your DLLs can visit sites that have collections of books in other languages, to support literacy learning.

When watching videos, make sure you interact with the videos and the children just as you would when reading a book to them. Think Vygotsky: You are the knowledgeable other scaffolding your learners to a greater level of understanding. You are aware of what the children know and can make connections to the new content. Stop the video at strategic points and deconstruct what is happening. Focus on your target vocabulary. Make sure to ask questions of increasing difficulty. Think back to Bloom's taxonomy, which promotes higher-level thinking. For example, after asking children what they *remember* and *understand* about a video clip on taking care of a pet, ask them how they might *apply* that information if they own pet.

Remote or virtual learning situations are challenging for all young children and their families, and perhaps especially so for young DLLs. One issue can be access to technology and Wi-Fi. If you need to provide remote lessons, survey the families of your young learners to make sure they have the technology they need. This could best be accomplished at the beginning of the school year when you are obtaining other information. Many school systems and communities have programs that refurbish and donate computers, tablets, and smart phones to students. Once you know your students have the technology, they may need help securing Wi-Fi. Even if a child has Wi-Fi at home, it may not always be reliable due to the number of people in the home using it. Research the area where your students live, and find free hot spots. Many public libraries provide hot spots outside the building so that Wi-Fi can be accessed even if the building is closed.

Once you know your students have the devices and conductivity they need, create lessons for them. Use and replicate what you know is developmentally appropriate for young children. Use the theory and strategies in this book to help you meet the needs of DLLs with real-time (synchronous) or recorded (asynchronous) lessons and at-home activities.

Use Your Resources

As the teacher of record, you will always be responsible for your students' learning—no matter what additional supports you may have. Still, using the resources at your school can be a great help in reinforcing a child's learning. If you teach in an elementary school, the media, reading, and ESOL specialists can help you tremendously. Let them know what you are teaching, and ask them for ideas about how to support your DLLs. If you are teaching in a preschool, think about surveying the families in your class to see what resources they can bring to your class. They may be able to provide translation or to volunteer an hour or two a week to give you an extra pair of hands so you can give all the children extra attention and support with language development.

Reach out to resource teachers, families, coworkers, and community members with specific requests for assistance. The more they know about what you are teaching and the abilities of your students, the better they will be able to assist you. Each school and school system uses these specialists in different ways. Some will work in your room; some will pull the children out. Communication is key. Let them know what you are teaching so they can preteach and reteach as needed. Find out what they are teaching so that you can reinforce this in your own classroom. Finally, seek professional development (PD) to help build your skills. Administrators are often in search of meaningful PD for their teachers. Suggest that this be one of the topics for everyone. Perhaps a group of educators at your school or within your school system could engage in a community of practice focused on meeting the needs of DLLs. After determining the exact outcomes, the group could conduct a book study (for some excellent resources, see appendix B) or invite a professor from a local college of education to give a presentation followed by time for discussion, planning, and implementation for what has been learned. The group could then conduct peer observations and provide feedback to one another.

Ask, ask, and ask again for help. You are not in this alone, and no one teacher can know everything no matter how long she has been teaching. Find someone at your school who knows the resources available at your school and/or community and the best person to approach to get the most appropriate answer to your question. This applies to assistance with teaching strategies as well as assistance with getting to know the unique cultures of your students.

Find resources online. Use the theories in this book to help you evaluate the source of the resources and to select resources that will best support your unique students. Appendix B will give you some ideas of where to start.

If possible, seek an international experience for yourself where you are immersed in a different culture and language. Rather than taking a guided tour or a cruise where you are surrounded by people like you who speak English and where you are seamlessly guided from place to place, consider a trip where you are immersed and need to navigate alone or in a small group. It is enlightening to have the experience of securing food, finding a bathroom, and reserving a place to sleep in an unknown context where you are not fluent in the language. Some organizations in the United States offer service trips in which participants go to other countries to build schools or assist with curriculum development. This is one way to get an immersive experience; however, beware that you do not approach this experience from a colonial perspective, meaning that you are going to "save" people. Rather, approach the experience with the mindset that you are going to learn much, much more than you will give. I have had the privilege of being on several trips of this nature and have been humbled by how much I have learned. Experiencing firsthand what it is like to not understand the language or customs has informed my practice as a teacher more than most of the other training I have had.

For many of us, traveling out of the country is not an option, so you could seek an immersive experience without even leaving the country. Find out where there is a linguistic enclave in your own area, and attend a cultural event or go shopping. Being immersed in an unfamiliar culture will help you get a glimpse of what your students are experiencing—and will lead you to have more empathy and ask more questions about a child's culture.

Making Connections

DLLs are an asset in your classroom. Not to oversimplify, but many teachers have found DLLs to be models of resilience, positive attitudes, and infectious persistence (Rivera, Waxman, and Powers, 2012). The strategies used to differentiate lessons for DLLs, especially in an early childhood classroom, are often examples of developmentally appropriate best practice for all students. The experience of working with DLLs will also help English-only learners to be ready to work in the global workplace. By learning alongside children from different backgrounds, they will be able to take on different perspectives, which will help them with problem-solving and critical-thinking skills.

Hopefully this chapter has given you some strategies based on learning theory and second-language acquisition theory that you can adapt for your own students and classroom. Remember that you are not getting rid of everything you have been doing in the past; you are just shifting your practice to better support your DLLs as well as the rest of the children in your class. As we move to chapter 4, we will discuss how to support and connect with the families of our DLLs.

Working with Families of Dual-Language Learners

One of the essential elements necessary to meeting the needs of young learners is a positive working relationship with their families. The families of young DLLs are no exception, and in fact may be in extra need your special care and concern. What follows are some strategies for working with families of DLLs. You will notice these may be essential when working with your students who are English-only speakers as well.

Get to Know the Backgrounds of the Families

The first step to creating positive relationships is getting to know the backgrounds and cultures of the families and students you serve. Reach out to families you have previously worked with and people in your community who can give you insight into these cultures. For example, find teachers or administrators at your school or a nearby school who have worked with children from the same backgrounds as the families of your students. Or reach out to local organizations or places of worship who work with and serve the communities of these families.

When you meet with your cultural-resource connections, you will need to bring a list of questions. Do not stop at asking what languages the families speak or the name of the country of origin; those details are just the beginning of their important story. Ask questions such as the following:

- What is the school system like in the family's country of origin? What materials were available? How long was a school day? a school year?

- What were the academic expectations for each grade level?

- What is the political climate like?

- What is the geographic climate like?

- What religions are practiced in the family's country of origin?

- What are some of the unique customs of that region?

If your community resource knows the families personally, ask about the occupations of the family members in their country of origin. Are they the same as their occupations now? Sometimes, when a person moves from one country to another, certification or licensing for some occupations do not transfer with him. For example, a family member may have been an attorney or physician in his country of origin but may be working in construction now due to the inability to speak English and/or the US or state licensing requirements. Also ask about the school system in the family's country of origin. For example, in El Salvador, the school year starts in February and ends in late October, and many students do not go to high school if they cannot afford bus money.

If possible, find someone who immigrated and/or was a DLL as a child who would be willing to talk with you about his experience. Ask around your school. You may be surprised to find a colleague who was a DLL as a child and can provide insight into what that experience was like.

One characteristic we tend to shy away from in school settings in the United States is religion. It is important to find out the religious backgrounds of all your young learners (not just DLLs) so you can understand their beliefs and how they may affect your teaching. For example, students who are Jehovah's Witnesses do not celebrate birthdays or holidays such as Halloween or Thanksgiving. Many religions, such as Roman Catholicism and Islam, observe times of fasting, although young children are not required to do so. The majority of immigrants to the United States cite religion as very important (58 percent). Most immigrants (68 percent) identify as Christian, but immigrant populations also include those who are Muslim (4 percent), Hindu (4 percent), Jewish (1 percent), and Buddhist (1 percent). Only 20 percent of immigrants come to the United States with no religious affiliation at all (Pew Research Center, 2014).

As you gather information and learn about the families' cultures and countries of origin, beware of overgeneralizing. By interacting with individuals who understand your students' cultures or have been DLLs themselves, you can gain a fuller understanding of each of your students as unique. There may be some common patterns within countries and cultures; however, no two families or individuals are alike. And of course, no two experiences are alike! Avoid viewing one person or one family as representative of an entire country or culture. Don't identify an individual from a certain place as the spokesperson or "poster child" for everyone from that country or background. This is true of English-only children as well. Just because a student is from California does not mean that he can surf and knows movie stars (assumptions made of my children by other children when we moved from California to Maryland). A child from Texas might or might not have lived on a ranch (or have seen a real cow, for that matter). The United States is large and diverse; so are other countries and cultures. Use the information you gather as a starting place to find out even more information about the families and to develop empathy and sensitivity for the students in your classroom. By taking the time to get to know your students, you will help them feel more included and safer in your classroom.

Build an Understanding of Cultural Customs

Ask about specific practices and customs that might inform your teaching. Cultures differ, for example, in how children and adults are expected to interact, how people view time, and how parents interact with schools and teachers. In certain countries it is impolite to look in the eyes of a person in authority, so for a teacher to demand that a child look her in the eye would be disrespectful. The concept of time and timeliness can vary from country to country (or region to region within a country). Find out from your cultural insiders what the concept of time is in that culture, and plan accordingly. In schools in the United States, events start for the most part exactly when the schedule says they should start. For example, if Back to School Night is scheduled to start at 7:00 p.m., it will start at 7:00 p.m. on the dot. In other cultures, this may not be not the case. Seven o'clock may be the time people start to show up; the event may start minutes or even hours later. In the United States, parents are expected to help their children with homework. This is not true in all cultures. Some parents do not know they are supposed to help with schoolwork at home. Some cultures have a high regard for teachers and believe that the teachers will teach the children and the parents are not worthy of teaching them. Parents may not ask you for assistance. If this is the case, explain to parents that they are their child's first teacher, that they are qualified, and that they need to help their children at home.

Explain conventions and expectations of your classroom explicitly to the parents so they know what to expect and exactly how they can help their child meet with success. You need to be proactive and support the parents, even when they do not ask. Developing cultural sensitivity to these issues, rather than making assumptions about behavior, will help both you and your students in the long run.

My father was a teacher at a high school near a university. Over time, he grew accustomed to teaching the children of professors who were visiting from other countries, and he became familiar with many of their customs. On the evening of his first Back to School Night, some parents were seated in his classroom at the appointed starting time, but many more were not in attendance. He looked into the hallway, where he found some parents waiting. It turned out they were from China, where it would be disrespectful to enter a classroom before being asked to enter by the teacher. From then on, he knew to check the hallway and to explicitly invite parents into his classroom.

Consider Implicit Bias

Over the past few years, you may have heard the term *implicit bias,* meaning the unconscious prejudice and stereotypes we all have and may act on without intending to (Brownstein, 2019). People can have implicit bias on any number of characteristics, such as gender, race, or sexual orientation. Research conducted on the implicit bias of teachers towards DLLs reveals that, while most teacher express positive beliefs about their DLLs, their implicit beliefs may be more negative. For example, a teacher may be very welcoming of DLL students, but during instruction time, the teacher might not call on the students who are learning English, or might rush to provide answers rather than provide scaffolding to DLLs to strengthen their critical-thinking skills. We need to reflect on our own practice to understand how possible implicit bias may play out. If we know the best practices for DLLs but do not closely examine our possible implicit biases, then we are at risk of not employing these practices to the best of our ability (Harrison and Lakin, 2018). You may want to engage in a conversation with another teacher—someone with whom you can be honest—to discover any biases you may have. You then could invite this person to observe you in action to see if there are patterns in how you interact and treat children. Not all behavior fueled by implicit bias is negative on the surface. Some teachers' biases lead them to feel sorry for children due to their tumultuous immigration experience. Consequently, these teachers may not expect enough from them academically; such low expectations can compromise those students' academic achievement.

Develop Empathetic Practice

By learning as much as you can about your young DLLs and their families, you will be able to walk in their shoes, come to a deeper understanding of their perspectives, and act with empathy (McGowan, Christenson, and Schoenberg Muccio, 2020). An empathetic perspective will help you not become frustrated by behavior that does not meet your expectations. Learning leads to empathy.

For example, when I was teaching first grade in a suburban elementary school with a large DLL population, half of whom were refugees, a two-year-old child escaped from his house nearby. His mother was an immigrant and did not speak English. At lunch, the staff room was buzzing with comments about this child and his mother, but I was surprised by who were the most judgmental: the teachers who did not have children of their own. Before this conversation, I thought the parents in the room would be more judgmental of this situation. However, as a parent myself, I had empathy for the toddler's mother. In spite of the best parenting, things can still go wrong. None of the parents in the staff room were immigrants; however, we could empathize with the toddler's mom. Parenting was the common experience we shared, in spite of the fact that the context of our parenting was likely very different.

The lesson here is that we can find common ground with families and can empathize by connecting to those characteristics we have in common. And with empathy we can try to put ourselves in the shoes of the families and children when we encounter characteristics that we do not have in common. For example, you may not have left your extended family behind in another country, but you probably have had to be absent from someone you love at some point in your life. How did that separation make you feel? Now imagine that you do not have the resources to visit your loved one in the near future or at all. What would that feel like? Or at dinner tonight, take a moment to think about what you are eating. It is no doubt something familiar. Now imagine that on your plate is something you have never seen or tasted before. At first it may be new and exciting, but how would you feel as the days went by? You would probably be homesick for familiar foods and a familiar environment, even if the home you had left offered no opportunities or was dangerous. We all long for the familiar. While you may never have the experience of leaving your home behind, you can be empathetic by learning more about your students and their families and trying to place yourselves in their shoes.

Immigration Status and Your DLLs

Under federal law, all children—no matter their legal status—have the right to a public education. It is illegal to conduct federal raids at schools or to share information protected under Family Educational Rights and Privacy Act (FERPA) laws. Schools are a safe place where every child is to be cared for and is legally allowed to be. Why? Because Immigration and Customs Enforcement (ICE) cannot legally conduct raids or use the school system in any way to detain children or their families (ACLU, 2020). As teachers, it is our job to help students feel safe and welcome in the classroom. The best way to help these children is to remain empathetic to their situation and to provide whatever resources you can to them and their families.

Remember, the majority of DLLs in US early childhood education were born in the United States. Thus, it is uncommon to have an undocumented student in class (US Department of Education, 2019). Children's family members most likely also have legal status, but some may be undocumented. Until a person officially becomes a US citizen, his legal status can change. For example, a person could come to the United States as a refugee, and after some time the US government could suspend that status; then the person would need to return to his native country.

The most vulnerable DLL students you may encounter are those with refugee status. The United States has a long and mostly proud history of accepting refugees, and these children and families left their home country to escape natural disasters, war, violence, or persecution (UNHCR, 2019). Another term you may encounter is *migrant*. In some areas of the United States, some children who are DLLs may be in migrant-education programs, meaning their families work in agriculture and the jobs (and their residences and schools) move with the ebb and flow of the harvest.

Develop Relationships with Families

Build relationships with the children and their families by learning not just generalities about culture but also about their personal details. By taking an interest in the children in your classroom's families, they will know that you are invested in them. When you are authentically invested in them, they will be more invested in your classroom as well.

Learn common greetings in each family's L1. Make yourself vulnerable as you struggle with pronunciation, to demonstrate that it is acceptable to make mistakes as a normal part of the learning process. This may encourage the families to be vulnerable with you and to feel comfortable using their emerging English skills.

Contact families early in the school year, and make that initial contact positive. When sharing information with families, always start with their child's strengths. All children have strengths. By contacting parents first and making it a positive experience, they will be more inclined to approach you with questions or concerns.

A child's primary caregiver may be one of any number of people: one or both biological parents, grandparents, aunts or uncles, other extended family, or community members. Some children and their families have been traumatized by violence or disaster in their home countries. Due to these circumstances, sometimes children are in the United States without their parents and are living with other relatives. Or perhaps the children were living with other relatives and have now been reunited with their parents after months, or in some cases, years. These families are facing the challenge of getting to know each other all over again. Whoever is responsible for a child is the person you will be establishing a relationship with.

Arriving in a new country is stressful, and it takes time for families to become settled. Sometimes children have many responsibilities at home, such as helping with younger children or assisting their families financially by helping in a family business. They may not have time to complete assignments out of school. In some cases, parents lack education or literacy in their native language, so they cannot help with concepts reinforced in the homework. They can, however, help reinforce their native language at home, which will provide the foundation for English language learning. Be creative with homework assignments, and allow students to complete them at school under your guidance. Also consider that, due to highly mobile living or working situations, some students may not be able to come to school every day. Do not judge a student's journey through the education system, but rather celebrate each day the student is able to attend your class.

The primary goal of your communication is to help the families build connections to your classroom. Through your relationship with them, you will encourage them to come to school, to not be afraid, to understand that school is a safe place, and to know that in the United States it is customary for families to be present at school to interact with teachers at conferences and events. Let them know that you and the staff at your school are there to help their children, so they can always ask for help and resources.

Once you build relationships with the families of your DLLs, they will be able to trust you and know that you are doing your best for

The following is a quote from a colleague of mine whose children did not speak English when she moved to the United States.

"The fact that the child does not speak English does not mean that the child is not intelligent or cannot think. Be curious about the child's cultural and linguistic background, and find out what he or she knows and understands. Also, learn some key phrases in the child's home language to make the child comfortable when he or she first enters your class."

their child and will be able to support what you are doing in the classroom. Without your support, they will not be able to follow up or know what to do. Often people come to the United States to have more opportunities for their children. They know the importance of doing well and understand that working hard in school is the gateway to their children's success. As a team, you and the families can make this a reality.

Create a Learning Environment that Celebrates Diversity

Invite all families to share their cultures with the class. This is important to make all children feel included and to develop their cultural competence, while also helping them learn more about their own identities. Exposing English-only families to DLL families, and vice versa, will also help break down cultural stereotypes. Provide all your students with "mirrors"—materials and lessons that reflect their specific cultures—and "windows"—materials and lessons that expose them to the other cultures in the world (Style, 1988). Their families can help you do this.

Mr. Seth is a teacher in a half-day preschool program located in rented space in a church. In addition to children from the local area, his class includes children from China whose parents work in the local tech industry. He also has three students from Afghanistan who live in local refugee housing. When the church members, who are not affiliated with the school, heard there were children in the refugee center who did not have access to preschool, they took up a collection to pay their tuition for the current school year.

To support a unit on fairy tales, Mr. Seth invited the families of his students—with the help of a translator at the refugee center—to bring in their favorite fairy tale and read it to the class in their native language. He recorded the readings with the class tablet. Some parents were not able to come to school, so they sent in videos from their smart phones. The local library provided books in English, Farsi, and Mandarin. As a result, Mr. Seth's students were exposed to a rich selection of fairy tales that Mr. Seth himself did not know existed. He now has a library of videos that he uses as part of his literacy centers. Through participating in this event, all the families felt valued, and the children benefited from listening to stories that were mirrors of their cultures and windows on the cultures of others.

Communicate with Families

Just as you do with your English-only families, make an effort to communicate regularly with the families of your DLLs. Use all the forms of communication that you use with the entire class and then adapt a few. Think of layering communication, meaning that, rather than relying on one form, such as your ClassDojo, use several methods. For example, send home old-fashioned paper notes just in case a family cannot access technology. Many people can access social media via their smart phones, so take advantage of that tool. If you are at a school where the families drop off and pick up their children, make sure to meet parents before and after school at least several days a week, if not daily, to connect with families in person. If available, you could have the translator(s) join you on occasion to help translate these informal conversations. This is a tip for administrators as well. One of the principals I worked with set aside time in his calendar to be at the drop off/pick-up area of the school to connect with parents. He said that proactively building relationships with families helped to avoid problems and, in the long run, saved him time and created a nurturing environment for everyone.

Develop routines around communication so that parents learn when to expect communication from you. Think about sending home communication on Friday, to sum up the week and lay out expectations for the week ahead, in both paper and electronic forms, so busy families will have time to digest the information over the weekend. Then, follow up with a brief reminder

Identifying Home Languages

By law, all families must fill out language surveys upon registering at any public school; many child-care facilities and private schools require this as well. Sometimes known as the Home Language Survey, this instrument helps schools identify DLL students and, in the case of public schools, starts the process for testing to see what level of English (if any) the children have acquired. This is not a test of legal status, nor is it allowed to be presented to immigration services. It is solely for educational purposes. You should let parents know that if they decline to take the survey, they may be declining additional educational resources for their child. As indicated by the United States Department of Education (2018), student information forms must include questions such as:

- What language(s) is (are) spoken in your home?

- Which language did your child learn first?

- Which language does your child use most frequently at home?

- Which language do you most frequently speak to your child?

- In what language would you prefer to get information from the school?

for the week ahead on Monday, via both technology and paper. And do not underestimate the power of a phone call in building relationships with families.

Be succinct in your communication, and avoid using idiomatic language and jargon. Use simple, straightforward language to communicate your most important points. Think about having someone (perhaps someone who does not work in an educational setting) read over your information to make sure it is clear.

Always translate any information you send home. Some schools have access to translators in the most frequently spoken languages. However, you will need to build in lead time to give the translators time to do the translation. Try to add to your resources people in the community who can provide translation. Sometimes local social clubs or churches in linguistic enclaves can be a resource. If you do not have translators at your school or in all the languages your children speak, you can use online translation tools. Just be sure to add a disclaimer, because online tools are not foolproof. Keep in mind the level of the parents' native language and write to that level—but without being patronizing.

In addition to paper and electronic communication, set up both informal and formal times to meet with the children's families. Engage a translator for this in-person contact; many districts have them or, if one is not available, ask someone from the community. In less optimal cases, find an older student who speaks both languages. As a last resort, ask the child or a sibling to translate. It's not ideal to rely on the child or a sibling, because this can set up an unhealthy power dynamic in the family where the child, and not the parent, is in charge of the situation. Once families see that you want to engage with them, they often will bring their own translators along to both formal and informal gatherings.

Encourage Family Participation in Events at School

Families of DLLs may need extra encouragement to participate in school events, not because they do not care (as I have often heard some teachers say) but because they simply do not know what is expected of them. Clearly communicate exactly what the event is, how their children are expected to be involved, what their children will gain from participating in the activity, and exactly what will be expected of the families during the event. For example, the Spring Fling may be a longstanding tradition at your school, and no explanation is needed for those who have been involved. They already know that this is the premiere social event of the school year and that the proceeds from the class-run carnival games pay for the assemblies for the next school year. They know that the items for the bake sale need to have a spring theme and be homemade. All of this hidden information needs to be explicitly described and explained in your various forms of communication. Do not forget to explain these types of events in minute detail to your students, as well. Once families know the expectations, they will be set up for success.

Depending on your school culture, families are often invited and sometimes expected to volunteer in the class. Create unique opportunities for all families based on their strengths. Volunteering should not always equate to donating supplies or money. Create tasks in your classroom that do not require fluency in English. For example, you could invite parents who are not fluent in English to work in their native language with students who share that language.

Identify and remove barriers to participation. Teachers commonly complain of low attendance by families of DLLs (some English-only families too). There may be several reasons for the low attendance. If the event was well-advertised using translation and layered of means of communication, attendance might have been poor because work schedules or lack of transportation was a barrier. Perhaps families need child care for siblings. Maybe the events are scheduled during family mealtimes. Money might be an issue. Brainstorm the barriers and then build bridges to overcome them.

One school discovered that many families of DLLs had members who worked the night shift: an evening event was not optimal because these workers were just getting up and preparing for their work day. The school found that offering events first thing in morning yielded better attendance because family members were able to come right after they got off from work. The Family Sunrise Breakfast Story Time became very popular.

Sometimes we expect families to come to meetings without their children. Often this is not possible, because families do not have the resources to hire a babysitter or do not know anyone they can leave their children with. Invite the children, and offer child care provided by someone the children know. You and your fellow staff members can set up a place for the children and rotate the responsibility for this duty. While some of you are meeting with parents, others can care for the children. Or think about including the children as part of the meeting. For example, if you plan on offering a workshop on fostering literacy or math skills, having the children attend is excellent strategy. You could show the families and children how to read books together or play math games, and they could practice before going home.

Is transportation a barrier? Sometimes children are bused to schools that are not close to their homes, and families do not have a way to get to the school. Think of holding the gathering at an alternate site closer to their homes, such as a community center or public library. Is food a barrier? Are the families expected to attend during mealtimes? If that is the case, plan on providing food, and make sure you advertise this fact. Is money a barrier? If you are charging admission or the event is a fund raiser, some families may not be able to afford to attend. Think of asking for optional donations instead of a set admission price.

What else could be a barrier in your unique setting? Have a brainstorming session at your next staff meeting. Think about the potential barriers to participation, and come up with some possible solutions to these barriers. With a little creativity, many of the barriers can be overcome or mitigated. Be creative and flexible when offering school events. When is the best time for your families? Ask them. You may have to change what you have done in the past, but it is more important to change a tradition and have people attend than to maintain a tradition and have no one there. Maybe the times the families have available are so fragmented that one all-encompassing event is not possible. In that case, think of offering several smaller events at various times. Yes, it is more work, but remember what your goals are: connecting with families and meeting the needs of the children.

Support Families in Maintaining Their Home Languages

The most important advice you can give the families of DLLs is to encourage them to help their child maintain and grow in their native language. Encourage families to speak their richest, most academic language to support their children's learning. Remember what we learned in chapter 2: a strong foundation in one's L1 creates a strong foundation for one's L2. A strong native language will yield a strong second language, and a rich understanding of conceptual knowledge and academic vocabulary in the first language builds a strong foundation for developing that knowledge in the second language. In most cases, teachers do not have the resources to provide native-language support, so the families will have to do that for you.

Suggest that families check out books and possibly other materials in their native languages from the local public library. Determine ahead of time what languages and resources are available. Be sure to explain to the families where the library is, how to check out books, and that this process is free. Research online resources, and share these with your families. Some families do not have access to computers, but many people have smart phones on which they could connect with resources.

By including the languages of your children in your classroom, families will know their language is of value and that they are an important and necessary resource for their child's school experience. One parent of a DLL student offered the following tips for working with families of DLLs.

Parents want their children to be successful and may view English-only as the way to success, often at the expense of the child's home language. Do not allow this to happen. The home language is the foundation for the child to learn a new language. The home language is vital for the child's self-identity and social development. It helps the child remain connected with the parents and elders. Depriving the child of his home language is breaking the bond between the child and his family. So make sure to encourage the parents to continue emphasizing the use of the home language with their child.

Making Connections

First and foremost, have empathy for your students and their families, both DLLs and English-only speakers. Learn what you can about the cultures of your students, but make sure you do not overgeneralize. Be careful to not make judgements and be transparent about your implicit biases. As early childhood educators, we have the obligation and opportunity to learn about our students and to break down our biases so that we can serve children and their families in the best way we are able. Now in chapter 5, all we have learned will come to life. Join me in Ms. Emily's classroom as she teaches a unit on how things change.

Bringing It All Together: A Unit of Study in a Kindergarten Classroom

This chapter is an illumination of the shift in practice to make instruction more effective for both DLLs and English-only learners in a typical kindergarten unit of study. Here we will weave together what you already intuitively knew with ELL learning theory covered in this book. We will explore the lesson through the lens of the teacher making the instructional decisions. As you read, remember: this process is unique to each teacher and each class of students; it is not a recipe. This is just a launch pad for your own ideas. You know the children in your class better than anyone else and are equipped with the conceptual knowledge of best practices for ELLs *and* English-only speakers. This is a shift in practice—not throwing out everything you know and starting over!

Ms. Emily's Classroom

Welcome to Ms. Emily's kindergarten classroom, located in a town right outside a large urban center. Although it's not a Title I school, 31 percent of her students qualify for free or reduced lunch. Nine of the twenty-four students are DLLs. Six languages are spoken; the largest group is comprised of Spanish speakers, and the next-largest group is made up of Hindi speakers. Some of the families work in the local procurement warehouse for a large national company.

Ms. Emily taught at a private preschool (about one-third of the students were DLLs) for three years before starting at her current school, where she has been for the past six years. At this school, she taught second grade for two years and prekindergarten for two years; this is her second year teaching kindergarten. Ms. Emily did not have any coursework as an undergrad on second-language acquisition theory and strategies. She has attended several workshops offered by her current school, reads what she can in journals for teachers, and has picked up a lot of strategies on the job from other teachers.

The Unit

"How Things Change" is a standard science and social-studies unit for kindergarten. The curriculum guide for the school system had this unit planned for the month of February. Knowing that children learn best through authentic learning experiences and hands-on activities, the first needed adjustment was to move the unit to a time of year when changes can best be observed by the teacher. Therefore, Ms. Emily moved this unit to the end of March, the time when the air turns warmer, the leaves bud on the trees, and the forsythia blooms in her region. Her students are able to observe and experience changes firsthand.

After initial discussions with the children about the concept of change, Ms. Emily decided to enrich the study by embracing the students' interests. She showed the children a video about change and read several books to them. Then, the students stated they were most interested in plants and the changes they go through. Thus, the unit embraces the basic concept of change and then goes into specifics about the change from winter to spring, how infants change from birth to age five, and finally, about how seeds grow to become plants. Where and when possible, teach units when they make the most sense and when students can make authentic connections. Ms. Emily decided to focus on the change of seasons; however, if you live in an area where the weather does not change as dramatically, try connecting to the concept of change in a different way.

Because Ms. Emily had already researched the backgrounds of her students, she was able to support the concepts in this unit with culturally relevant materials. She provided books on childhood representing her students (in her case China, India, and Honduras) and in the children's native languages (Mandarin, Hindi, and Spanish). In addition, she selected culturally appropriate books on the changes of seeds and plants.

Her instructional day includes a flow of lessons from whole group to small group. Each of her lessons is a combination of homogeneous and heterogeneous groups, depending on the specific skill she is teaching. In addition to whole-group instruction, Ms. Emily meets with all children once a day in small groups. The majority of the time she groups the children homogeneously around their levels of English language arts or math skills. These groups are not static. She reconfigures them frequently based on her assessment data. Small-group time is when children read at their instructional level and learn phonics, decoding skills, and math concepts appropriate to their individual needs.

A Word about Themes

This unit is an example of how to select a theme for a unit and then authentically incorporate it into the children's learning. An inauthentically incorporated theme (bears, for example) would be using bear counters in the math area, gluing bear cutouts on the calendar, and making a craft project in which the children uniformly glue googly eyes on precut bear heads. An authentic bear theme, on the other hand, would be one in which children learn about the habitats and habits of bears, hear books about bears, and see videos of real bears and fantasy bears, and then compare and contrast them. They use their knowledge of bears to turn the dramatic play center in to a den for the winter so they can "hibernate." Ms. Emily could have used the topic of bears to teach the concept of change, if the children had showed an interest in bears.

Start with a concept from your required curriculum and then teach it through the lens of a theme based on the children's interests. Find and solve problems through the lens of the theme.

Content Areas

English Language Arts

Read Alouds

Ms. Emily read a few books (both narrative stories and expository books) and showed a video about change. Then, based on the class discussions, she refined the study to the children's interests: How plants change, how winter changes to spring, and how I change. She then selected books for read alouds on those distinct themes.

For each subtheme, she selected six to eight academic vocabulary words from the books and videos. She will use these words as a focus for her discussions and center activities throughout the three-week unit. In addition, she selects books at the listening level of the whole class (not the children's reading level) to ensure the texts lend themselves to the development of higher- order critical-thinking skills.

Before reading aloud, Ms. Emily previews all her books, and she scripts her comprehension questions ahead of time. She keeps Bloom's taxonomy in mind so that her questions are of increasing rigor. She looks at her state's standards and makes sure she is focusing on the required elements of literature, such as plot, characters, and setting, and elements of informational texts, such as text features (lists, headings, boldfaced words, captions, and so on), so that her young learners are prepared to deconstruct texts of various structures.

During the read aloud, she calls on students strategically by giving them questions she knows they are able to answer. For an ELL child just coming out of the silent period, she asks surface-level questions—Where is the cat?—and has the child point to an answer in the book. For the English-only learner or ELL with CALP in English, she asks questions that require the children to make logical inferences based on the information provided in the book. For example, she might ask, "Why did the cat leap out of the window?" Ms. Emily has taught her class the strategy of turn and talk during a read aloud. Turn and talk involves Ms. Emily posing a question to the entire class. The children then turn and talk to the person next to them to answer the question. This way, everyone gets a turn to discuss the question. After a minute or two, depending on how engaged the children are in answering the question, she brings the group together and calls strategically on individual students for their answers. Ms. Emily modeled and had the children practice this strategy many times before they could use it effectively. She is also strategic in how she pairs the children. Sometimes she partners children with the same L1 so they can discuss in rich detail; other times she partners an ELL with a child who speaks only English so that the English-only child can be an English role model.

Poems

Ms. Emily also selects a poem of the week to go with each unit of study. For this unit, she will select three poems. On the theme of children changing between birth and age five, she uses *Now We Are Six* by A.A. Milne as a resource. She selects simple, illustrated poems that foster phonemic awareness, phonics, and concepts of print. She decides what to focus on by consulting her state's English language arts curriculum. She sends the poems home each week in English, and with the help of Google Translate (with a disclaimer stating the source of the translation) in the languages of her ELLs. This is an effective way to keep families updated on the topics of the units of study so they can provide support in their L1 at home. The poems are also tools for families to learn English.

The children participate in a shared reading of the poem daily, and on Friday they perform the poem for the class across the hall. This learning activity helps build fluency. For this week she selected the classic poem "The Wind" by Christina Rossetti. March is a windy month in the area where Ms. Emily's school is located, so the children can observe firsthand how wind can create change on a breezy day. The poem provides rich vocabulary that the children can easily understand from the context and by acting it out.

The Wind

Who has seen the wind?

Neither I nor you;

But when the leaves hang trembling

The wind is passing through.

Who has seen the wind?

Neither you nor I;

But when the trees bow down their heads

The wind is passing by.

Math

The curriculum for math during the time of this unit is a review of one-to-one correspondence, counting from one to twenty, a review of writing the numerals 1 through 12, and nonstandard measurement with objects, such as blocks and hands. She introduces the children to standard measurement with rulers, measuring tapes, and scales.

Ms. Emily incorporated these goals in her whole-group math instruction and, after assessing her students, she grouped them by skill level in these areas to reteach for children who needed more practice and to extend for those who had already mastered the material. The ELL students were spread across the groups because they were grouped by their ability in math and not by their ability in English. For independent practice, Ms. Emily modeled the activities in the dramatic play center (see pages 81-82). There the students practiced writing their numbers and measuring "patients" with measuring tapes and a scale. Just like a pediatrician, they recorded the data they collected on their patients.

Social Studies

The topic of children changing and growing over time is also part of the social studies curriculum for the year. Because the children were interested in this topic at this time and it fit with the overall theme of change, she moved the topic to this unit. Ms. Emily included authentic cultural connections throughout the unit, both to reflect the children in her class and to be a window to the cultures of the world. She did this through her careful selection of books and videos and her choice of realia, in this case the seeds and leaves for the science

Working with Specialists

Ms. Emily is very fortunate as she has an ESOL teacher who pulls out her ELLs for thirty minutes every day and also comes into her class three days a week for thirty minutes. The school does not have dedicated planning time for the general-education teacher and ESOL teachers. However, Ms. Emily seeks the ESOL teacher during her planning time or before or after school to keep the ESOL teacher updated on her curriculum and to share the main points of a unit and materials. In turn, the ESOL teacher shares the curriculum she covers when she pulls the ELLs from the class. Ms. Emily then knows what to reinforce with the children back in her classroom. During center time three times a week, the ESOL specialist meets with the ELL students to preteach and reteach skills and academic vocabulary. Sometimes Ms. Emily adds an English-only learner to the group, if the ESOL teacher is covering a skill or concept the child needs assistance with. In the case of this unit on change, the ESOL teacher is focusing on the academic vocabulary of the unit, the names of numbers in English, and the English vocabulary necessary to measure and weigh an object. Ms. Emily and the ESOL teacher are a team working on mutual goals with their DLLs.

center. Ms. Emily celebrates cultural connections by illuminating various holidays during the year; however, she always makes sure to embed these cultures and traditions whenever possible in all units to ensure that her students know that recognizing everyone's culture is important all the time, not just on one day of the school year.

Learning Centers

Center activities should reinforce concepts taught in whole group and should be a time of collaboration. There are many ways to group children for centers. Sometimes you may wish to group them by their ability levels. Other times, you will want groups of a variety of levels or groups who will work well together without the assistance of adults. Set up the centers with communication in mind. If possible, centers should be places where children interact and learn from one another while reinforcing concepts they have mastered independently. (Think Vygotsky!) Remember, children learn from social interactions and from a knowledgeable other. Children can be the knowledgeable others for one another, especially when learning languages. By creating and modeling tasks for children to work on together, they can interact and learn from each other. For this unit, Ms. Emily has grouped the children heterogeneously by skill level and by level of English. She has also paid close attention to grouping children harmoniously, matching children who work well together.

Writing Center

In the writing center, Ms. Emily provides a variety of writing materials, such as pencils, pens, and different types of paper, as well as word cards from the previous week, with photographs of course! The students use these word-picture cards to fill in sentence starters or to create their own stories or expository texts. Of course, Ms. Emily knew to model this for the whole class before having the children practice on their own.

Dramatic Play

When discussing the children's journey from birth to the age they are now, the children talked about going to the doctor for checkups. Based on this interest, Ms. Emily converted the dramatic play area to a doctor's office complete with a pretend doctor's bag containing toy replicas of the tools of the trade and a real stethoscope. She provided materials, such as small plastic funnels, plastic tubing, and tape, and picture directions so the children could make their own stethoscopes. Ms. Emily covered the shelf with paper and made outlines of the tools. She wrote the name of each tool in the outline so the children can clean up after themselves and to help them start reading these words. This dramatic play center also functioned as the math center for the three weeks of this unit, as the math curriculum was focusing on measurement. In the doctor's office, Ms. Emily included a measuring tape, a real scale to measure baby dolls that represent the children in the class, and some stuffed animals too. Ms. Emily had demonstrated how to measure and weigh the "babies," and the children were going to practice and record the results in the babies' medical records. Ms. Emily created medical-record sheets where the children wrote the name of the baby, how many ounces the baby weighed, and the child's length in inches. To support the writing skills, each baby was labeled with his or her name. Ms. Emily also posted a number chart with directional arrows to remind the children how to write their numbers.

She also read books about visiting a doctor and the importance of medical care. She provided writing materials to write "prescriptions" and give directions to the families of the babies as well. The children were encouraged to interact with other children in any language they would like. Ms. Emily noticed that some of the English-only children picked up a few words in Spanish, Mandarin, and Hindi.

Book Corner

Ms. Emily has a core book collection of classics of western children's literature, as well as a collection of books that reflect the current topic. The classics are there so the children will develop familiarity with these examples of western literature. Many modern stories and plot lines are based on the classics, and if a child is not familiar with those, the child will not understand the new iteration or will miss the cultural touchpoint that the classic book represents. The book corner also includes both literary and information texts on changes in plants, in seasons, and in children as they grow from newborns to five-year-olds. The collection is a window to the world and a mirror reflecting the cultures and backgrounds of all the children in her class.

How Plants Change

The Amazing Life Cycle of Plants by Kay Barnham

From Seed to Plant by Gail Gibbons

How a Seed Grows by Helene J. Jordan

How Plants Grow by Dona Herweck Rice

Lola Plants a Garden by Anna McQuinn

The Patchwork Garden/El pedacito de huerto by Diane de Anda

Sophie's Squash by Pat Zietlow Miller and Anne Wilsdorf

The Tiny Seed (English)/*Xiao Zhong Zi* (Chinese)/*La semillita* (Spanish) by Eric Carle

Tops and Bottoms by Janet Stevens

Underground by Denise Fleming

How Seasons Change

Abracadabra, It's Spring by Anne Sibley O'Brien

Because of an Acorn by Lola Schaefer and Adam Schaefer

Changing Seasons by Sian Smith

Everything Spring by Jill Esbaum

Exploring Spring by Teri DeGezelle

In the Middle of Fall by Kevin Henkes

Snow Rabbit, Spring Rabbit: A Book of Changing Seasons by Il Sung Na

Watching the Seasons by Edna Eckart

How Children Change

Babies Don't Eat Pizza by Diane Danzig

The Brother Book by Todd Parr

Growing Up With Tamales/Los tamales de Ana by Gwendolyn Zepeda

Lola Reads to Leo by Anna McQuinn

Moony Luna/Luna, Lunita Lunera by Jorge Argueta

Oscar va a la escuela grande/Oscar Goes to Big School by Lee Kilby

Otto Goes to School by Todd Parr

The Sister Book by Todd Parr

Books in Spanish, Chinese, and Hindi

Bulbul Ka Bacha: A Baby Nightingale (Hindi edition) by Professor Qayyum Nazar

Dian (The Dot) (Chinese) by Peter Reynolds

Famous Jatakea Tales in Hindi by Manoj Publications Editoral Board

Guachipira va de viaje (Guachipira Goes on a Trip) (Spanish) by Arteaga Quintero

Maisy's Food /Los Alimentos de Maisy: A Maisy Dual Language Book (Spanish and English) by Lucy Cousins

Marisol McDonald Doesn't Match /Marisol McDonald no combina (Spanish and English) by Monica Brown

Panchtantri Ki Lokpriya Kahniyan: Timeless Stories for Children in Hindi by Wonder House Books

Block Center

All year long, the block center is filled with a supply of Legos and wooden blocks of various shapes and sizes. The blocks are stored on shelves that are labeled with the outlines of the blocks and the names of the shapes inside the outlines. On the wall, Ms. Emily has posted a chart of the shapes and the names in English, Hindi, Mandarin, and Spanish. She rotates additional materials and realia in the block center, depending on the theme and time of year. This keeps the area fresh for children and helps them discover new problems to solve. Because spring had arrived, she replaced the toy snow-removal equipment and mounds of snow (cotton balls) with toy farm equipment designed for tilling and preparing the soil for planting. She had read both realistic fiction and informational text to the children about this process as part of her discussion on winter changing to spring and seeds changing to plants. She included multicultural examples of the planting process. She put the books she read in the block center for reference and inspiration, along with word-picture cards of the academic vocabulary: *till, sow, soil, tractor,* and *farmer.* She has provided four cards representing different genders and cultures with the word *farmer* on each.

Art Center

Over the course of the year, Ms. Emily invites the children to experiment with a variety of art materials, such as water colors, tempera paint, colored glue, and tissue paper. This month she has provided pastels and various sizes of drawing paper next to the easels. The featured artists of the month are Gu Kaizhi (ca. 344–406), a Chinese landscape painter, and Winslow Homer (ca. 1836–1910), an American landscape painter. She selected prints of *Nymph of the Luo River* by Kaizhi and *Boys in a Pasture* by Homer to post in the art center. Ms. Emily read biographies about the artists and showed the children the specific techniques each artist used. The students were invited to try using pastels to draw landscapes of winter turning to spring. Ms. Emily helped the artists interactively write descriptions of their masterpieces. Each child had a turn, during whole-group time on different days, to share her picture and read—with Ms. Emily's assistance, if needed—what had been written. Through their art explorations, the children were building fine- and gross-motor skills, academic vocabulary, concepts of print, and phonics skills. DLLs were successful at this cognitively demanding activity because it was complex with cues. (Think Cummins's quadrants.)

Science Center

Ms. Emily has created a matching game in which the students use their investigative skills and tools, such as magnifying glasses and a microscope to match seeds and leaves. She was able to locate five real examples. After the children make their matches, they check their work by opening a box in which she has glued seeds to the corresponding leaves and labeled each pair. Posted near the science center is the map that Ms. Emily used to show the students where the seeds they were studying originated.

Outside Environment

For the focus of their weekly nature walk, Ms. Emily showed the children how winter was changing to spring over the course of the unit. She grouped her students in triads and gave each group a check sheet of the vocabulary words (with pictures) so they could check them off as they went. Not everything could be found the first week because some things, such as buds on the trees, had not yet emerged. It was not until the end of the three weeks that the children could find everything. Each week, they recorded observational data just like scientists and talked about the changes they were observing. The ELLs were able to be engaged because they were working in heterogeneous groups, they could observe the changes firsthand, and the worksheet was supported by visuals.

Communicating with Families

Ms. Emily sends home a short weekly newsletter summarizing the curriculum covered during the week and looking ahead to the next week. With the help of the school translator (or Google Translate in a pinch) she provides the newsletter, both on paper and on the school website, in the children's home languages. She includes the poem of the week and the academic vocabulary being covered. In this way, families can support this learning at home in their L1.

In addition, she gives a weekly homework assignment. As part of the study of change from birth to age five, she asked each family to fill in a template titled "_____'s Journey from Birth to Now." The family filled in information about each year of their child's life:

birth, age one, age two, age three, age four, and age five. The families were invited to fill in each square with a photo, a drawing, and/or a couple of sentences describing their child at that age. The families were invited to use their L1 and were given the entire three weeks of this study to complete this homework. The children brought these projects back to school and shared them as they were able. This engaging and developmentally appropriate homework helped the children and families feel part of the classroom community. Ms. Emily invited the school translators to help her translate the ones written in Hindi, Mandarin, and Spanish. She displayed the children's templates on the bulletin board in the hallway outside the classroom.

Shifting Your Unit Planning

Now that you have had a glimpse into Ms. Emily's unit on change and her planning process, how will you shift your teaching to serve the needs of the ELLs in your class and to maximize the learning of your English-only learners? Check out the list below, as it may help you with your planning process. A blank unit planning guide is provided in appendix A on page 91.

Sample Unit Planning Guide

Name of Unit/Theme: Birds

Shifts for DLLs

Main concepts to be taught: Characteristics of birds, principles of flight, everyone needs shelter

Connections to Required Curriculum: Throughout this unit, children develop phonemic awareness, concepts of print, one-to-one correspondence, and evaluation skills from the science standards

- **Emphasize academic vocabulary:** Instead of lists of isolated words, provide lists of words relevant to your theme and strategically teach them throughout the unit. For example, if your unit is on birds, you can provide words and pictures of the following terms: *bird, nest, fly, flight, egg, beak, feather, perch*, and the names of local birds.

- **Model and think aloud:** Throughout the unit, model and think aloud every step of the way. For example, during interactive writing verbally describe what you are writing and how you are forming letters and developing your thoughts. During a read aloud, stop to ponder what is written and what the pictures are about, and make predictions. Model and think aloud every activity and routine that you will expect your students to perform alone. This will be an ongoing practice; you will need to repeat and have the children practice after you model until they can do it alone.

- **Select books, videos, realia, and visuals to teach new concepts:** Research books on your theme—both narrative and informative—and make sure they include your targeted academic vocabulary. Collect and use realia if at all possible, and provide pictures and videos that reflect your theme. Remember to stop and ask questions when viewing videos.

  » Narrative books: *Ruby's Birds* by Mya Thompson, *Bird Count* by Susan Edwards Richmond, *Are You My Mother?* by P. D. Eastman

  » Informational books: *Bird Watch* by Christie Matheson, *Birds, Nests, and Eggs* by Mel Boring, *About Birds: A Guide for Children* by Cathryn Sill

  » Realia and/or visuals: bird's nest, feathers, egg, photos of different types of birds' nests, photos of birds, realistic stuffed birds, birdseed

- **Highlight authentic cultural connections:** Include resources that reflect the cultures of all the children (mirrors) and that give all children an experience of cultures different from their own (windows). For example, include birds from cultural contexts represented in your class as well as from around the world. Compare and contrast the similarities and differences.

  » Mirrors for unit on birds: photos of birds common in India, China, Honduras, and the United States; online recordings of variety of bird calls to reflect the cultures of all of the children in your class.

  » Windows for unit on birds: photos of birds common in India, China, Honduras, and the United States; online recordings of variety of bird calls so all the children in your class experience and learn about the wider world around them.

- **Provide hands-on learning activities:** In addition to reading and viewing videos and photos about the theme, engage children in hands-on activities. For example, after reading a book about birds' nests, build a nest with the children and discuss characteristics of effective nests.

Provide materials, such as pine straw or hay, twigs, and thin paper strips in your science or art center, where the children can construct their own nests. Give them an opportunity to share their nests with others and discuss how the construction of their nest is effective.

Go on a bird walk with the children. Invite them to listen for bird calls and to try to spy as many birds as they can in the local area. When you return to the classroom, ask the children to turn to a partner and talk about what they saw and heard.

- **Set up independent activities in centers that are extensions of the learning concepts:** For example, set up materials for the children to use to make their own bird feeders to take home. You could provide clean, empty milk cartons; cardboard; glue; twine; scissors; paint and paintbrushes, or permanent markers; birdseed; and ziplock bags. The children can work together to cut holes in the sides of their cartons, glue on little roofs made of cardboard if they like, decorate their bird feeders, and tie on a loop of twine at the top. They can take their feeders and a small bag of birdseed home. Provide instructions to parents about filling the feeders with the birdseed and hanging them where the children can see the birds that visit.

  In a whole-group lesson, you could show the children paintings and photos of birds from the Audubon Society. Then in the art center, you could provide images of some bird paintings and photos as inspiration for the children's art work.

  In the listening center, you could download or provide online access to recordings of bird calls for the children to listen to. For example, https://www.bird-sounds.net/ offers recordings of North American bird species. You can also find bird calls on YouTube.com. Provide photos of the birds that are recorded, so the children can match each bird with its call.

- **Seek additional classroom support:** Think about who can help with this unit. Do you have an ESOL specialist? an instructional aide? a parent with expertise or strong interest in birds? a local nature expert who could visit the classroom to talk about birds? Ask them to come to the classroom to support the children's learning about the unit topic.

- **Support the families in exploring this unit with their children:**
  There are lots of ways to support families in participating with the unit topic. For example:

  » Offer visuals via your class newsletter.

  » Translate materials on the unit topic to send home.

  » Let children borrow books about birds to read with their families.

  » Invite the families to the classroom to see what the children have been learning or to hear a local bird expert.

  » Provide website urls so families can explore birds together.

Making Connections

Hopefully, part of this book was a review of what you know and thus validated your knowledge. You have learned something about the research behind second-language acquisition and some practical strategies to incorporate in your classroom. With the basic concepts of ELL theory and strategies at hand, you can now explore additional resources. Appendix B gives you some places to start. As you know, the art and science of teaching is a journey and we all, no matter how long we have been teaching, continue to learn and add to our tool kits. Sometimes, those of us who work in the early childhood field are surrounded by other teachers and administrators who do not know best practices for the children who are dual-language learners, and we find our ideas being challenged. Be confident that what you know is valid, and use the resources in this book to support your best practices.

The following are primary takeaways:

- **Demographics and statistics:** Most (typically 82 percent) of the young ELLs in your early childhood class were born in the United States and are citizens. Not all Spanish-speaking ELLs are from Mexico. Every child has the legal right to an education. It is illegal to deny education to ELL students.

- **The basic learning theories of second-language acquisition:** There are two levels of language skills: basic interpersonal communication skills (BICS), which take up to two years to acquire, and cognitive academic language proficiency (CALP), which take an additional three to five years to acquire. We also learned about Cummins's common underlying proficiency (CUP), which explains that a child's L1 supports learning an L2.

- **Classroom strategies:** In many cases, a slight shift in instructional practice will help you serve your DLLs: lots of hands-on learning activities, modeling, thinking aloud, and use of realia and visuals. These strategies also serve English-only learners.

- **Connecting with families:** Get to know everything you can about your students and their families so that you can serve them with empathy. Do not make assumptions about them by the way they look or where they are from. Encourage families to continue teaching their L1 at home. A strong L1 is a strong foundation for learning an L2 and leads to L2 CALP. Think outside the box, and implement family-involvement activities that maximize the potential for participation for all families your serve, both ELL and English-only. What are the barriers to attending? Find out and remove them.

ELLs are an asset in your classroom. Their presence will help prepare all your students to become global citizens and take their places in the increasingly global workplace. Do your own research to learn more about the culture of others. We all have culture—what is yours? If possible, seek experiences with other cultures: travel abroad or visit a linguistic enclave where you are the one who does not speak the L1 of the community. Absorb how it makes you feel and what steps could have been taken to make you feel comfortable. Then, bring that knowledge back to your practices in your classroom.

All children deserve a classroom where they feel safe and secure and free to learn and grow.

Never forget that *you* know the children in your class and *you* have the tools to adapt instruction to meet their needs. The foundational work of wonderful early childhood educators like you give all children the start they deserve.

Appendix A: Unit Planning Guide

Name of Unit/Theme: _____

Shifts for DLLs

Topic/Unit: List the main concepts to be taught. _____

_____

What if any additional background knowledge will you need to provide? _____

_____

_____

Connections to Required Curriculum: _____

_____

_____

- **Emphasize academic vocabulary.** Words for this unit/theme:

  _____

  _____

  _____

- **Model and think aloud.** What I will model/think aloud to support this unit/theme?

  _____

  _____

  _____

- **Select books, videos, realia, and visuals to teach new concepts.**

  Books/videos for this unit/theme: _____

  _____

  _____

  Narrative/literature: _____

  _____

  _____

  Informational: _____

  _____

  _____

Gryphon House
www.gryphonhouse.com

Realia and/or visuals for this unit/theme: _____

_____

_____

- **Highlight authentic cultural connections (mirrors and windows).**

  Mirrors for this unit/theme: _____

  _____

  _____

  Windows for this unit/theme: _____

  _____

  _____

- **Provide hands-on learning activities.**

  Hands-on activities for this unit/theme (list at least one for each concept to be
  taught): _____

  _____

  _____

  Independent center activities to support this unit/theme: _____

  _____

  _____

  Field trips, guest speakers, and so on to support this unit/theme: _____

  _____

  _____

- **Seek additional classroom support.**

  Whom can I ask for help with this unit/theme? How can they help me? _____

  _____

  _____

  Support the families in exploring this unit with their children.
  How will I support families with this unit/theme (newsletters, online links, books,
  other resources)? _____

  _____

  _____

What translations are needed and in what languages?_____

_____

Appendix B: Additional Resources

This book will get you started on your journey with your DLLs. Here are a few additional resources you may wish to check out, now that you have the basics. This list is not exhaustive. Have fun!

- **¡Colorin Colorado!** www.colorincolorado.org

  As the heading of the website states, ¡Colorin Colorado! is a bilingual site for educators and families of ELLs. This comprehensive site shares current information and offers a wealth of teaching tips and resources for teachers and families.

- **Head Start** https://eclkc.ohs.acf.hhs.gov/culture-language

  The Head Start website has a section dedicated to the needs of ELLs and their families. They have some excellent articles that extend some of the topics presented in this book.

- **International Children's Digital Library** http://en.childrenslibrary.org/

  This free website has a large collection of children's books in more than fifty languages. Some titles are translated in to multiple languages, and there is even a section on teaching tips. The books can be read on a tablet, projected via your computer, or copied for students to use in class or at home.

- **Language Castle** www.languagecastle.com

  This resource website is a conduit to helpful blogs, current newsletters, and publications to assist educators and families with young DLLs.

- **National Association for the Education of Young Children (NAEYC)** https://www.naeyc.org/

  NAEYC has many resources, including books, blogs, journal articles, and conference sessions designed to help early childhood educators meet the needs of young DLLs and their families. A digital membership costs thirty dollars ($30US).

- **National Association for Bilingual Education** http://www.nabe.org/

  This association offers resources, including weekly eNews, an annual conference, and institutes to provide support to educators working with DLLs. Check to see if your state has its own association for bilingual education. Washington, California, Massachusetts, and Florida do, and could be a local resource for you.

- **Teaching at the Beginning** www.teachatb.org

  This website has a collection of videos of best practices for ELLs in action.

- **WIDA** https://wida.wisc.edu

  The WIDA is a consortium of approximately forty US states, DC, several US territories, Department of Defense schools, and the Bureau of Indian Education. WIDA provides tools and support to help educators and multilingual learners succeed. Many jurisdictions belonging to WIDA adopt Can Do Descriptors and assessment measures. If you have an English for Speakers of Other Languages (ESOL) specialist in your school, she may be using these resources. WIDA holds an annual conference.

References and Recommended Reading

Ahmad, Shamsidar, et al. 2015. "Adapting Museum Visitors as Participants Benefits Their Learning Experience?" *Procedia: Social and Behavioral Sciences* 168(9): 156–170.

Alanís, Iliana, and Maria Arreguín-Anderson. 2019. "Paired Learning: Strategies for Enhancing Social Competence in Dual Language Classrooms." *Young Children* 74(2): 6–12.

American Civil Liberties Union. 2020. "FAQ for Educators on Immigrant Students in Public Schools." ACLU. https://www.aclu.org/other/faq-educators-immigrant-students-public-schools

Armon-Lotem, Sharon. 2010. "Instructive Bilingualism: Can Bilingual Children with SLI Rely on One Language in Learning a Second One?" *Applied Psycholinguistics* 31(2): 253–260.

August, Diane, et al. 2005. "The Critical Role of Vocabulary Development for English Language Learners." *Learning Disabilities Research and Practice* 20(1): 50–57.

August, Diane, and Timothy Shanahan, eds. 2006. *Developing Literacy in Second-Language Learners: A Report of the National Literacy Panel on Language-Minority Children and Youth.* Mahwah, NJ: Lawrence Erlbaum.

Banach, Natalie. 2005. "Ethiopians Make Home in L.A." *Daily Bruin*. https://dailybruin.com/2005/07/04/ethiopians-make-home-in-la/

The Bell Foundation. 2017. "Research from the 1970s Onwards: Jim Cummins." The Bell Foundation. https://ealresources.bell-foundation.org.uk/eal-specialists/research-1970s-onwards-jim-cummins

Bialik, Kristen, Alissa Scheller, and Kristi Walker. 2018. "6 Facts about English Language Learners in U.S. Public Schools." Fact Tank. https://www.pewresearch.org/fact-tank/2018/10/25/6-facts-about-english-language-learners-in-u-s-public-schools/

Bialystok, Ellen. 2001. *Bilingualism in Development: Language, Literacy, and Cognition*. New York: Cambridge University Press.

Blachowicz, Camille, Peter Fisher, Donna Ogle, and Susan Watts-Taffe. 2006. "Vocabulary: Questions from the Classroom." *Reading Research Quarterly* 41(4): 524–539.

Blakemore, Erin. 2019. "A Ship of Jewish Refugees Was Refused U.S. Landing in 1939. This Was Their Fate." History. https://www.history.com/news/wwii-jewish-refugee-ship-st-louis-1939

Blizzard, Brittany, and Jeanne Batalova. 2019. "Refugees and Asylees in the United States." Migration Policy Institute. https://www.migrationpolicy.org/article/refugees-and-asylees-united-states

Bloom, Benjamin, et al. 1956. *Taxonomy of Educational Objectives: The Classification of Educational Goals.* New York: Longmans, Green.

Boutte, Gloria S. 2002. *Resounding Voices: School Experiences of People from Diverse Ethnic Backgrounds.* Boston: Allyn and Bacon.

Breiseth, Lydia. 2015. "What You Need to Know about ELLs: Fast Facts." ¡Colorín colorado! https://www.colorincolorado.org/article/what-you-need-know-about-ells-fast-facts

Brownstein, Michael, Alex Madva, and Bertram Gawronski. 2019. "What Do Implicit Measures Measure?" WIREs 10(5): e1501.

Buysse, Virginia, et al. (2014). "Effects of Early Education Programs and Practices on Development and Learning of Dual Language Learners: A Review of the Literature." *Early Childhood Research Quarterly* 29(4): 765–785.

Cañado, Maria Luisa P. 2005. "English and Spanish Spelling. Are They Really Different?" *The Reading Teacher* 58(6): 522–530.

Cellania, Miss. 2014. "Autumnal Equinox Traditions." Mental Floss. http://mentalfloss.com/article/59049/autumnal-equinox-traditions

Cherry, Kendra. 2019. "Gardner's Theory of Multiple Intelligences." Verywell Mind. https://www.verywellmind.com/gardners-theory-of-multiple-intelligences-2795161

Christenson, Lea Ann. 2016. "Class Interactive Reading Aloud (CIRA): A Holistic Lens on Interactive Reading Aloud Sessions in Kindergarten." *Educational Research and Reviews* 11(23): 2138–2145.

Christenson, Lea Ann, and Jenny James. 2020. "Transforming Our Community with STEAM." *Young Children* 75(2): 6–14.

Christenson, Lea Ann, and Jenny James. 2015. "Building Bridges to Understanding in a Preschool Classroom: A Morning in the Block Center." *Young Children* 70(1).

Copple, Carol, ed. 2003. *A World of Difference: Readings on Teaching Young Children in a Diverse Society*. Washington, DC: National Association for the Education of Young Children.

Crawford, James. 2004. *Educating English Learners: Language Diversity in the Classroom.* 5th ed. Los Angeles: Bilingual Education Services.

Cummins, Jim. 1984. *Bilingual Education and Special Education: Issues in Assessment and Pedagogy.* Vol. 6. Multilingual Matters. San Diego: College Hill.

Cummins, Jim. 1991. "Language Development and Academic Learning." In *Language, Culture and Cognition*. Clevedon, UK: Multilingual Matters.

Cummins, Jim. 1994. "The Acquisition of English as a Second Language." In *Reading Instruction for ESL Students.* Newark, DE: International Reading Association.

Cummins, Jim. 2000. *Language, Power and Pedgogy: Bilingual Children in the Crossfire*. Clevedon, UK: Multilingual Matters.

Cummins, Jim, and Sharon McNeely. 1987. "Language Development, Academic Learning, and Empowering Minority Students." In *Bilingual Education and Bilingual Special Education: A Guide for Administrators*. Boston: College Hill.

De Valenzuela, J., and S. L. Niccolai. 2004. "Language Development in Culturally and Linguistically Diverse Students with Special Education Needs." In *The Bilingual Special Education Interface*. Upper Saddle River, NJ: Merrill/Prentice Hall.

Delacruz, Stacy. 2013. "Using Interactive Read-Alouds to Increase K-2 Students' Reading Comprehension." *Journal of Reading Education* 38(3): 21–27.

Echevarría, Jana, MaryEllen Vogt, and Deborah Short. 2004. *Making Content Comprehensible for English Learners: SIOP Model*. 2nd ed. Boston: Pearson Allyn and Bacon.

Fairfaxcounty.gov. n.d. "Languages Spoken at Home by Fairfax County Elementary Students." Fairfax County, Virginia. https://www.fairfaxcounty.gov/demographics/languages-spoken-home-fairfax-county-elementary-students

Fitzgerald, Jill. 2003. "Multilingual Reading Theory." *Reading Research Quarterly* 38(1): 118–122.

Fox, Mem. 2013. "What Next in the Read-Aloud Battle? Win or Lose?" *Reading Teacher* 67(1): 4–8.

Francis, David, et al. 2006. *Research-Based Recommendations for Instruction and Academic Interventions.* Practical Guidelines for the Education of English Language Learners series. Portsmouth, NH: RMC Research Corporation, Center on Instruction. https://www.centeroninstruction.org/files/ELL1-Interventions.pdf

Froude, Jenny. 2003. *Making Sense in Sign: A Lifeline for a Deaf Child.* Clevedon, UK: Multilingual Matters.

Frankfurt International School. n.d. "Second-Language Acquisition: Essential Information." FIS Community. http://esl.fis.edu/teachers/support/cummin.htm

Gardner, Howard. 1983. *Frames of Mind: The Theory of Multiple Intelligences.* New York: Basic Books.

Genesee, Fred, et al. 2005. "English Language Learners in U.S. Schools: An Overview of Research Findings." *Journal of Education for Students Placed At-Risk* 10(4): 363–385.

George W. Bush Presidential Center. 2020. A Nation Built by Immigrants. https://bushcenter.org/publications/resources-reports/reports/immigration.html

González-Bueno, Manuela, and Donita Massengill Shaw. 2011. "The Impact of Perception Training on ELL Spelling: Preventing L1 Phonetic Transfer." *Journal of Language Teaching and Research* 2(6): 1193–1203.

Graves, Anne, Russell Gersten, and Diane Haager. 2004. "Literacy Instruction in Multiple-Language First-Grade Classrooms: Linking Student Outcomes to Observed Instructional Practice." *Learning Disabilities Research and Practice* 19(4): 262–272.

Guerrero-Cruzado, Judith, and Judith Carta. 2006. "Assessing Vocabulary and the Bilingual Environment in Young Latino Children." *Perspectives in Communication Disorders and Sciences in Culturally and Linguistically Diverse Populations* 13(1): 8–13.

Guha, Smita. 2012. "It's More Fun Than It Sounds—Enhancing Science Concepts through Hands-On Activities for Young Children." *Teaching Science* 58(1): 43–47.

Hakuta, Kenji, Yuko Goto Butler, and Daria Witt. 2000. "How Long Does It Take English Learners to Attain Proficiency?" Policy Report 2000-1. Santa Barbara, CA: University of California, Linguistic Minority Research Institute.

Harrison, Jamie, and Joni Lakin. 2018. "Mainstream Teachers' Implicit Beliefs about English Language Learners: An Implicit Association Test Study of Teacher Beliefs." *Journal of Language, Identity, and Education* 17(2): 85–102.

Hewings-Martin, Yella. 2017. "Bilingualism: What Happens in the Brain?" *Medical News Today*. https://www.medicalnewstoday.com/articles/319642

Hill, Jane, and Cynthia Björk. 2008. *Classroom Instruction That Works with English Language Learners: Facilitators Guide*. Alexandria, VA: ASCD.

Hinchliff, Catherine. 2010. "Ethiopian and Eritrean Communities in Seattle." Historylink.org. https://www.historylink.org/File/9615

Huitt, William, and John Hummel. 2003. "Piaget's Theory of Cognitive Development." *Educational Psychology Interactive.* Valdosta, GA: Valdosta State University. http://www.edpsycinteractive.org/topics/cognition/piaget.html

Institute of Education Sciences, National Center for Education Statistics. 2018. "Local Education Agency (School District) Universe Survey Data, 2016–17." Common Core of Data: America's Public Schools. https://nces.ed.gov/ccd/pubagency.asp

Institute of Education Sciences, National Center for Education Statistics. 2019. "English Language Learners in Public Schools." The Condition of Education. https://nces.ed.gov/programs/coe/indicator_cgf.asp

Jones, Stephanie, and Suzanne Bouffard, 2012. "Social and Emotional Learning in Schools: From Programs to Strategies." Social Policy Report. *Society for Research in Child Development* 26(4).

Kaiser, Sue, and Greg Kaiser. 2012. "Lift-Off to the Common Core." *Leadership* 42(1): 8–11.

Kim, Sunha, and Mido Chang. 2010. "Does Computer Use Promote the Mathematical Proficiency of ELL Students?" *Journal of Educational Computing Research* 42(3): 285–305.

Kostelnik, Marjorie, et al. 2018. *Guiding Children's Social Development and Learning: Theory and Skills*. Boston: Cengage.

Krashen, Stephen, and Tracy Terrell. 1983. *The Natural Approach: Language Acquisition in the Classroom*. Hayward, CA: Alemany.

Learning Theories. 2014. "Bloom's Taxonomy." Learning Theories. https://www.learning-theories.com/blooms-taxonomy-bloom.html

Lee, Jung-Sook, and Natasha Bowen. 2006. "Parent Involvement, Cultural Capital, and the Achievement Gap among Elementary School Children." *American Educational Research Journal* 43(2): 193–218.

Litwin & Smith. 2019. "How Long Does It Take to Immigrate to the United States?" Litwin & Smith. https://www.litwinlaw.com/Articles/How-Long-Does-it-Take-to-Immigrate-to-the-United-States.shtml

McGowan, T. K., Lea Ann Christenson, and Leah Schoenberg Muccio. [under review.] "Fitting into Our Students' Shoes: An Exploration of Empathy in Early Childhood Teacher Education." *Journal of Research in Childhood Education*.

McLeod, Saul. 2019. "What Is the Zone of Proximal Development?" Simply Psychology. https://www.simplypsychology.org/Zone-of-Proximal-Development.html

Moore, Rob. 2004. "Cultural Capital: Objective Probability and the Cultural Arbitrary." Special Issue: Pierre Bourdieu's Sociology of Education: The Theory of Practice and the Practice of Theory. *British Journal of Sociology of Education* 25: 4.

Nagy, Tünde. 2018. "On Translanguaging and Its Role in Foreign Language Teaching." *Acta Universitatis Sapientiae: Philologica* 10(2): 41–53.

National Education Association. 2016. "Your Students and Immigration Raids: What You Can Do." https://www.nea.org/assets/docs/ice-raids-fact-sheet-1.pdf

National Geographic. n.d. "Vikings in North America: A Saga's New Chapter." https://www.nationalgeographic.org/

National Geographic. n.d. "Dia de los Muertos." https://www.nationalgeographic.org/

Pew Research Center, Religion and Public Life. 2014. "Religious Composition of Immigrants." Religious Landscape Study, Immigrants. https://www.pewforum.org/religious-landscape-study/immigrant-status/immigrants/

Pew Research Center, Hispanic Trends. 2015. "Modern Immigration Wave Brings 59 Million to U.S., Driving Population Growth and Change through 2065." https://www.pewresearch.org/hispanic/2015/09/28/modern-immigration-wave-brings-59-million-to-u-s-driving-population-growth-and-change-through-2065/

Psychology Notes HQ. 2018. "The Piaget Stages of Cognitive Development." Retrieved from https://psychologynoteshq.com/piagetstheory/

Radford, Jynnah, and Luis Noe-Bustamante. 2019. "Facts on U.S. Immigrants, 2017: Statistical Portrait of the Foreign-Born Population in the United States." Pew Research Center. https://www.pewresearch.org/hispanic/2019/06/03/facts-on-u-s-immigrants/

Ramirez, Naja F. 2016. "Why the Baby Brain Can Learn Two Languages at The Same Time." The Conversation. https://theconversation.com/why-the-baby-brain-can-learn-two-languages-at-the-same-time-57470

Rietveld, Christine. 2010. "Early Childhood Inclusion: The Hidden Curriculum of Peer Relationships." *New Zealand Journal of Educational Studies* 45(1): 17–32.

Rivera, Héctor, Hersh Waxman, and Robert Powers. 2012. "English Language Learners' Educational Resilience and Classroom Learning Environment." *Educational Research Quarterly* 35(4): 57–78.

The Room 241 Team. 2019. "Five Ways to Engage Parents of ELL Students." Resilient Educator. https://resilienteducator.com/classroom-resources/five-ways-to-engage-parents-of-ell-students/

Ross, Tracey. 2015. *The Case for a Two-Generation Approach for Educating English Language Learners.* Washington, DC: Center for American Progress. https://cdn.americanprogress.org/wp-content/uploads/2015/05/Ross-ELL-report.pdf

Sanchez, Claudio. 2017. "English Language Learners: How Your State Is Doing." NPR Ed. https://www.npr.org/sections/ed/2017/02/23/512451228/5-million-english-language-learners-a-vast-pool-of-talent-at-risk

The Share Team. 2018. "Five Stages of Second Language Acquisition." Resilient Educator. https://education.cu-portland.edu/blog/classroom-resources/five-stages-of-second-language-acquisition/

Simons, Gary F., and Charles Fennig, eds. 2017. *Ethnologue: Languages of the World*. 20th edition. Dallas, TX: SIL International. https://www.ethnologue.com/ethnoblog/gary-simons/welcome-20th-edition

Siraj-Blatchford, Iram, and Yeok-lin Wong. 2006. "Defining and Evaluating 'Quality' Early Childhood Education in an International Context: Dilemmas and Possibilities." *Early Years: An International Research Journal* 20(1): 7–18.

Staats, Cheryl. 2016. "Understanding Implicit Bias: What Educators Should Know." *American Educator* 39(4): 29–33.

Strutner, Suzy. 2013. "8 Cultural Differences between America and Other Countries." HuffPost. https://www.huffpost.com/entry/weird-cultural-differences_n_3875360

Style, E. 1988. "Curriculum as Window and Mirror." Nationalseedproject. https://nationalseedproject.org/curriculum-as-window-and-mirror

Teacher.org. 2020. "How to Teach Students about Holidays and History." Teacher. https://www.teacher.org/resource/teaching-holidays/

Terrell, Tracy D. 1977. "A Natural approach to Second Language Acquisition and Learning." *Modern Language Journal* 61(7): 325–336.

Turnbull, Blake. 2018. "The Potential Impact of Cultural and Educational Background on Foreign Language Teachers' Use of the L1." *Journal of Language Teaching and Learning* 8(1): 53–70.

United Nations High Commissioner for Refugees. 2019. "Refugee Resettlement Facts." U.S. Resettlement Facts. https://www.unhcr.org/en-us/us-refugee-resettlement-facts.html

US Department of Education. 2016. Digest of Education Statistics. National Center for Education Statistics. https://nces.ed.gov/programs/digest/d16/tables/dlt16 204.27.asp

US Department of Education. 2017. *English Learner Tool Kit for State and Local Education Agencies (SEAs and LEAs)*. Washington, DC: US Department of Education, Office of English

Language Acquisition. https://ncela.ed.gov/files/english_learner_toolkit/OELA_2017_ELsToolkit_508C.pdf

US Department of Education. 2019. "Our Nation's English Language Learners: What Are Their Characteristics?" Washington, DC: US Department of Education https://www2.ed.gov/datastory/el-characteristics/index.html

US Department of Education. 2020. "Developing Programs for English Language Learners: Lau v. Nichols." Washington, DC: US Department of Education, Office for Civil Rights. https://www2.ed.gov/about/offices/list/ocr/ell/lau.html

Vygotsky, Lev S. 1978. *Mind in Society: The Development of Higher Psychological Processes*. Cambridge, MA: Harvard University Press.

WIDA. 2012. *The English Language Learner Can Do Booklet: Grades 1-2.* Madison, WI: University of Wisconsin–Madison. https://wida.wisc.edu/sites/default/files/resource/CanDo-Booklet-Gr-1-2.pdf

Worrall, Simon. 2018. "When, How Did the First Americans Arrive? It's Complicated." National Geographic. https://www.nationalgeographic.com/news/2018/06/when-and-how-did-the-first-americans-arrive--its-complicated-/

Zoeller, Emily. 2015. "Below the Tip of the Iceberg." Center for Teaching for Biliteracy. https://www.teachingforbiliteracy.com/below-the-tip-of-the-iceberg/

Index